KNITTING

 *with*

DOG HAIR

KNITTING
with
DOG HAIR

A Woof-to-Warp Guide to Making Hats, Sweaters, Mittens and Much More

Kendall Crolius and
Anne Black Montgomery

ST. MARTIN'S PRESS
New York

Printed on recycled paper

Design by Kathryn Parise

LIBRARY OF CONGRESS CATALOGING-IN-PUBLICATION DATA
Crolius, Kendall.
Knitting with dog hair/Kendall Crolius and Anne Montgomery.
p. cm..
ISBN 0-312-10489-8 (pbk.)
1. Knitting—Patterns.   2. Animal fibers.   3. Hand spinning.
I. Montgomery, Anne.   II. Title.   III. Title: Dog hair.
TT825.C78   1994
746.9'2— dc20   93-42975
CIP

First Edition: March 1994
10 9 8 7 6 5 4 3 2 1

Contents

Acknowledgments

Special thanks to the following without whom this book could never have been written:

Barbara Binswanger and Jim Charlton, for their vision, their perseverance, and their HUGE bags of dog hair.

Patricia Crolius, knitter extraordinaire, for her indefatigable support, and especially for inspiring in her grateful daughter a lifelong love of crafts and needlework.

Many thanks for all their dogged efforts to Bob Weil, Becky Koh, Stephanie Schwartz, and Joe Rinaldi.

Pam Ramsey, Sheila Brodeur, and Kelley Brandt for spinning emergency supplies of dog yarn, and Detta Juusola for sharing dog yarn and her beautiful dog hair creations.

Jerie Lucas, a master spinner with a Certificate of Excellence from the Handweaver's Guild of America, for sharing her expertise in spinning dog hair.

Louise O'Donnell, the only master spinner in the U.S. with a C.O.E. in cat hair, for her valuable input.

The Handweaver's Guild of America, Inc. (2402 University Ave., Suite 702, Minneapolis, MN 55114; [612] 646-0802), a nonprofit organization "dedicated to upholding excellence, promoting textile arts, and preserving textile heritage," as well as educating the general public. The Guild hosts juried shows and awards Certificates of Excellence in both spinning and weaving. For a nominal membership fee, the Guild will put you in touch with a current member, who will serve as your "mentor" while you acquire your skills.

Ms. Sandra Bowles, editor of the Guild's beautifully produced *Shuttle, Spindle and Dyepot* magazine, for so generously taking photographs of Guild members' work and graciously referring us to valuable sources.

Our thanks to Hélène Rush, author of *The Knitters Design Sourcebook,* published by Down East Books in Camden, Maine, for permission to reprint the pattern for the Cardigan in Chapter Eight. We find this book to be a terrific resource, as it provides basic patterns in a complete range of sizes and, importantly, a variety of stitch gauges.

Our husbands and children, who cheerfully put up with dining room tables full of dog hair, and more take-out food than one should have to eat in a lifetime—we love you.

All the spinners we spoke with, who shared our passion for dogs and the gentle art of spinning, and who touched us so with their generosity and enthusiasm for our project.

And to Abigail, Irish, and Ollie. The Very Best Dogs.

PET HAIR DONORS

We received an outpouring of help from the exhibitors at the Spring 1993 Charlottesville-Albemarle AKC Dog Show. Most of the donors remained anonymous, kindly stuffing our self-addressed envelopes with pet hair and popping them in the mail. The following folks included their names: Amy Phaltz, Diane Swepston, Dyveke McCuhl, Joyce Ayotte, Harriet Gehorsam, Crystal Slaney, Donna Steckli, Liz Hanley, Debbie Goldstein, and Karin Slough.

Special thanks to Elizabeth Emanuel of Creatures Great and Small pet groomers; she provided fuzz from so many breeds and such a wealth of information, the book could not have been done without her.

Introduction

When we began *Knitting with Dog Hair*, most people thought we were a few puppies short of a litter, if not downright crazy. The exceptions were experienced spinners (for whom dog hair was merely another nifty fiber to experiment with) and people of exceptional vision and imagination (nearly all of whom owned beloved dogs who shed exasperating quantities of fuzz).

Kendall actually conceived of this project as she was spinning the hair of Ollie, a Great Pyrenees belonging to her friends Barbara and Jim. Like many spinners, she already knew that dog fuzz could be spun, since many books devoted to the craft of spinning carry a brief paragraph on it. But the information on dog hair is often sketchy and seems like an afterthought, a footnote to more substantial sections on alpaca, vicuña, and other exotic fibers. What was needed, she reflected, was a comprehensive compendium of information, complete with photos and diagrams, and, of course, an all-breed glossary of fuzz. Enter Anne, an avid recycler and dog maniac, who was heartily tired of shoveling fuzz bunnies the size of brontosauri into the trash. She interviewed legions of breeders and groomers, and sent countless bags of solicited fuzz to Kendall as spinning samples.

Kendall produced several miles of dog yarn, and an assortment of garments were knitted and then dispatched to eager dog owners, who now find themselves in pretty chic company. In fact, dog hair garments have been worn proudly by the rich and famous for generations. Vincent Astor sported a scarf knit by his wife, Minnie, from yarn made from their beloved poodle, Nora. Mikhail Baryshnikov reportedly pirouettes in a pair of leg warmers made from his dogs. And any pet lover can craft homegrown and handmade treasures by spinning and knitting with dog hair.

Spinning is a delightful and satisfying craft. It is quite simple to learn, but we realize not everyone will want to undertake it. For those of you who would love to knit with pet yarn, we have included a list of spinners who will spin it for you. And for those of you who are unable to find the time or inclination, some will even knit a garment from your beloved pet for you. But we do urge you to try it yourself. We think you will enjoy it immensely. We know you will derive enormous satisfaction from creating your pet hair clothing from scratch.

We do not profess to be the ultimate authorities on the craft of spinning. Kendall counts herself an amateur spinner (which Anne, who has truly terrible fine motor skills, thinks is excessively modest), and this book is written with the novice spinner in mind. But we were careful to interview as many dog-hair spinning experts as we could find, and we hope that even accomplished spinners will benefit from our experience and that of those we interviewed. This book was truly a labor of love, and we hope it gives you as much pleasure as the garments you create from your canine companion.

1

Why a Dog?

For millions of years, the human race has been living with and benefiting from its relationship with animals. We've relied on them for companionship, for transportation, for food—and for our clothing. The first garments our prehistoric ancestors wore to keep themselves warm in those chilly caves were undoubtedly animal skins. But those fashions required a onetime contribution on the part of our furry friends, not a particularly good deal from the animals' standpoint.

Several millennia later, our forebears figured out a way to make clothing from animals without killing them. Our ancestors learned that they could spin animal fibers such as wool into yarn and use the yarn to make clothes. This was not only a far more desirable method from the beasts' standpoint, it also established sheep as a renewable resource for wool instead of a one-shot source of skins.

History marches on, and not everyone has a backyard filled with sheep. But fear not! You too can make clothes from the critter in your life.

Putting on the Dog

Sheep don't have a corner on this market—fibers from the coats of all kinds of animals can be spun into yarn that can be used just as you would use store-bought yarn: for knitting, crochet, weaving, and a host of other crafts.

In fact, pet hair has characteristics that make it more desirable than wool. It produces a yarn that has a lovely "halo" of fuzz, much like mohair or angora. Though it is not as elastic, it is even warmer than wool. Susan Wallace, author of *Hair of the Dog*, made a hat of dog and goat hair that her husband wore while mountain climbing. He swears that it saved his life when he was caught by a sudden storm. The hat kept him incredibly warm, and although the wool hats worn by the rest of his climbing party became encrusted with ice, his hat remained completely ice-free!

While we can't guarantee that they'll save your life, clothes made from a critter you know and love are just so much more special than clothes from some anonymous sheep. What could be more delightful than wearing mittens from your Malamute, or a sweater from your Samoyed? Every knitter knows the feeling of satisfaction you get from wearing a sweater you've made yourself. Well, if you multiply that feeling about ten times you'll get a sense of what it's like to wear a sweater that was formerly Fido. Here are some basic points about making clothes from pet hair.

Cebe Wallace on the summit of Mt. Angeles in the Olympic mountains in Washington, wearing the dog and mountain goat hat spun and knit by Susan Wallace. He looks nice and warm. (Photo courtesy of Susan Wallace.)

Stop Vacuuming and Start Knitting!

One of the drawbacks of pet ownership is dealing with the problem of shedding. Most of us, out of loyalty to our pets, insist that they "don't shed much." Let's be honest—everything in your house is probably covered with a fine coat of pet hair. There are fur balls collecting dust under all the furniture. Well, fret no more! You can be proud to own a shedder once you take up pet spinning. All that fuzz that used to clog up your vacuum cleaner can now be put to good use. In fact, you'll probably want to brush your dog more often now—you'll not only have gorgeous new clothes but a better groomed pet and a cleaner house to show for it.

About Allergies

Dr. George W. Ward, Jr., Associate Professor of Medicine, Division of Allergy and Clinical Immunology of the University of Virginia in Charlottesville, Virginia, has the following comment about allergies: "First, let me say that allergies to dogs are far less of a problem than allergies to cats. It would appear that the allergies are from the dander shed from the dog's skin as well as the dog's saliva. Thus, thorough washing would probably remove most of the allergenic material, although a controlled study to answer this question has not been done."

Presumably *you* are not allergic to your own dog, but we don't recommend using petspun in gift items without checking with the recipient first, and we caution against using dog yarn for baby clothes.

On the other hand, Kendall's brother Tucker is allergic to wool but comfortably wears a hat made from his beloved dog, Tsagun. Dog yarn may be an excellent substitute for your friends who can't wear wool.

A Global Phenomenon

Some research revealed what we suspected—other cultures have been recycling Rover for centuries. On a recent trip to Estonia, dog-hair spinning expert Jerie Lucas discovered a woman selling dog-hair sweaters at a village market. Through the auspices of a gifted interpreter, Ms. Lucas discovered that, according to the local folklore, dog hair alleviates symptoms of arthritis and rheumatism. And while we make no such claims, Ms. Lucas subsequently toured an Estonian mill devoted to spinning a combination of dog hair and wool, which certainly indicates that there are some true believers out there.

Susan Wallace discovered that spinning dog hair was once quite common among tribes of the Pacific Northwest. Although the craft has died out, Susan was able to create a dog-and-goat headband for a Nootka Indian to wear during a three-day initiation ceremony. He was delighted to be able to wear a piece of traditional regalia that no one had worn for three generations.

What Will the Neighbors Say?

We admit it—when you first tell your friends that the garment you're wearing was previously worn by your dog, you're bound to get some raised eyebrows, not to mention a few shrieks of horror. But after they've had a chance to get used to this revolutionary idea—and when they notice how lovely a garment it is—it won't be long before they're leaving bags of dog hair on your doorstep in the hopes that you'll spin for them.

The Craft of the Nineties

We believe that spinning and knitting with pet hair could become the new national craze. Just think about it—it's the perfect craft for our times.

It is very economical. Talk about something for nothing, this is a way to get clothes from stuff you used to throw out! (Now if we could just figure out something to do with dryer lint. . . .) The tools you'll need to start spinning are quite inexpensive, and some can even be made at home. Of course, you may ultimately want to invest in a full array of spinning equipment, but it's not necessary until you really get hooked on spinning pet hair.

It is good for the environment. We don't have a clue how much pet hair ends up in our landfills and incinerators, nor do we know how much electricity is used vacuuming pet hair, but we suspect it is quite significant! Going from garbage to garment by using the pet hair that would otherwise be discarded is, in fact, a very creative form of recycling.

It is certainly kind to animals. Spinning and knitting with pet hair is a way to get a fur that you can wear with absolutely no guilt at all. And your pet is bound to appreciate all the extra attention he's going to get—the extra grooming and the extra appreciation from his owners and their friends.

It reinforces family values. This is a craft that the whole family can participate in. The kids can help brush the dog, and older kids can help prepare the fibers for spinning. It's a terrific way to spend time together.

So start casting on with that cast-off fuzz!

2

Collecting the Raw Material

The first step in the journey from dog to garment is to get the hair from the animal. As any owner of a shedder knows, separating the dog from the hair is a process that is all too simple. However, some dogs are more cooperative than others.

It is the rare dog owner who doesn't know precisely when, and precisely how much, his or her pooch sheds. Exclamations range from the rather smug "Oh, he's no trouble at all" to "Is it snowing or is Friedrich blowing his coat?"

First-time or oblivious dog owners should note that most breeds shed at least twice a year: a substantial shedding in the fall, and a truly impressive shedding in late spring. (Among certain breeds, this phenomenon is known as "blowing one's coat," a metaphor that barely captures the sudden, copious, and precipitous nature of the shedding process.) During shedding season, some double-coated dogs, like the Bouvier des Flandres, will adorn one's floor with clumps of fluff the size of small puppies. (Assuming one hasn't bred one's Bouvier recently, it's safe to deposit these balls in a paper bag for storage.) Single-coated dogs, such as Beagles, tend to scatter their hair pretty much throughout the year.

No matter what the season, we have found that black dogs can be trusted to shed on a light surface and light dogs will be drawn to your favorite dark couch. This seeming perversity on the part of your pet is merely his (or her) way of reminding you that a serious grooming is in order. And though one can—and should—collect pet fuzz all year long, one does not want to miss the dog's natural shedding cycle, when the harvesting is truly wonderful.

While picking up the stray fuzz balls that float under the furniture is perfectly appropriate, you will stand a better chance of a good harvest if you make a concerted effort to take the fuzz directly off the animal.

Rule number one is that you should never shear, cut, or shave fur from your pet if those procedures are not part of his regular grooming. Not only would such a radical approach seriously humiliate your companion and render him exceedingly unattractive, it is counterproductive. To spin a really nice yarn, you need the longest, softest fibers your pet can grow. (However, some dogs, such as Poodles, which are used to being clipped into assorted topiarylike shapes, don't mind being shorn in the least, and their long, soft clippings can be spun—see the "Harvesting Pet Clippings" section for further instructions.)

Harvesting Pet Brushings

Happily, the best way to harvest fuzz is also the most pleasurable for you and your dog: a good, thorough daily brushing, particularly in shedding season. The only tools you really need, which are available in most pet stores, are a rounded-tip, high-quality stainless steel comb and a slicker brush. The slicker brush boasts a large, flat surface studded with short,

Anne's daughter Jessica hugs her Bouvier puppy, Lucy, after a grooming. (Janis Jaquith, photographer.)

angled metal bristles. It works well on all types of coats, and collects long hair without damaging it. Dogs with thick, cottony, or woolly undercoats can be partially stripped with a comb or a gizmo called a "rake," which, unlike the slicker brush, is capable of getting right down to the skin and will yield awe-inspiring quantities of fuzz. (One groomer we worked with stripped a Newfoundland who was blowing his coat and nearly filled a lawn-and-leaf bag in one sitting.)

We do advise you to start with a dry animal. He or she doesn't have to be any cleaner than usual, because you will be washing the fur either before or after you spin it. In fact, it's probably *not* a good idea to wash your pet before collecting the fur, because: (a) you're going to have to collect fur over days, weeks, or perhaps even months, and we suspect you won't want to give your pet a daily bath; (b) you shouldn't store the collected fur when it is damp because it can mildew; and (c) if your pet is a cat, she will really take a dim view of any bath she doesn't give herself. (We understand that show cats are an exception to the "no baths, thank you" rule, but it certainly holds true for every self-respecting house cat we know.)

To begin, brush your dog gently, with long, smooth strokes. This will ensure both efficient collection of fuzz and an ecstatic pet. Only the most suspicious dog will suspect that you have an ulterior motive. Your average trusting pet will assume that all of this extra attention is simply another expression of your utter devotion to him. Do not burst his bubble. Your pet will be even more appreciative of you as master or mistress. You'll not only get all the fuzz you could ever need, you'll get a better groomed and more handsome beast in the bargain.

If your dog is one of those pups for whom grooming is the canine equivalent of Chinese water torture, we have some helpful hints: food, food, and more food. Your dog will be much easier to groom after he has ingested a heavy meal. The soporific effect of an especially generous ration of kibble will help him relax. (This is not the time to feed your pet unusual or unaccustomed treats, however, especially if he has a delicate digestive system. Anne made that mistake with one of her Bouviers, Zeko the Wonder Dog, and nearly asphyxiated him.) Anyway. Bribing your pet with familiar treats is a time-honored training tool, and will help your pet view grooming with a less jaundiced eye.

If you are desperate for a batch of fuzz and it is not your pet's regular mealtime, we strongly recommend exercising him into a state of near catatonia. This works especially well with puppies, who tend to squirm under the best of circumstances.

We also find it helps to talk to your pet throughout the grooming process, praising him when he behaves and consoling him through the rough spots.

When all else fails, we like a little soft music to settle our nerves.

As we will discuss in chapter 10, coats vary substantially from breed to breed. While some dogs, such as Afghan Hounds or Yorkshire Terriers, offer long, soft, silky hair that can be harvested from almost any part of the body, others have coats with substantial textural differences: hair from around the face, for example, might be a good deal coarser than the long, soft, more spinnable fibers found in the belly region. In double-coated dogs, it is the rich trove of fluffy, cottony, or woolly undercoat that spins the nicest yarn.

As you brush your pet, you may need to pause from time to time to pull the accumulated pet fur from the brush. Place it carefully in a bag or a bowl to keep Rover from rolling in it in his ecstasy . . . it's exceedingly inconvenient to brush the same old fur puffs off his body a second or third time.

After you've given your pet the once-over twice, you will probably have harvested most of the fur available at one sitting. You may want to brush him for a few more minutes just to be nice.

Harvesting Pet Clippings

If you ordinarily groom your pet by clipping him, the clippings can be spun if they are fairly long—about two to three inches in length. Clippings do not produce quite as soft a yarn as brushings, because the cut end of each hair tends to be a bit stiff and will stick out from the finished yarn, so the yarn will be a little scratchier. But we *have* spun very nice yarns from Poodle and Bichon Frise clippings, so don't let your clippings go to waste—your groomer may temporarily question your sanity when you ask him to save Fido's fuzz, but when you show off your finished sweater, you may well be inundated with clippings from every dog in town!

Harvesting "Sprinkles" from Short-Haired Breeds

Short-haired breeds such as Boxers won't yield fuzz that is spinnable on its own, but you can collect the hair to blend with wool or the fibers from a longer-haired breed. Brushing is the best way to collect these fibers, called "sprinkles," and while some sprinkles will stick in the brush, we recommend that you groom the pet on a clean sheet to collect as many of these precious fibers as possible. This is admittedly a labor-intensive and time-consuming process, but for owners who are determined to wear something from their short-haired beloved, it can be well worth the effort.

Special Harvesting Instructions for Cats

If you are a cat owner, you may need to try an alternate method of fur harvesting. When cats groom themselves, they remove many of the loose fibers from their coats, as any cat owner who has been awakened in the middle of the night by the sound of the cat hacking up a hairball can wearily testify. As a result, there may not be much fuzz left for you to harvest. (And no, there is no way to salvage the cat hair from a hairball to spin it.)

We know some cats, such as Calamity and Jazz in Michigan, who are quite happy to be combed, and the harvest from these particular longhairs is absolutely lovely. But some other cats we know, such as Faulkner, Hadley, and Emily in California, deeply resent anyone attempting to take over their grooming responsibilities (perhaps California has produced an entire genetic line of cats who simply resist combing!). And though we have spun some samples taken from the "California Cats" under protest, their owner, Anne McGrath, has devised an alternate harvesting method, which she calls "housecleaning."

Instead of using the vacuum cleaner, Anne prowls the house, brushing all of the furniture with one of those Velcro-type lint brushes. She insists that knowing that you're collecting

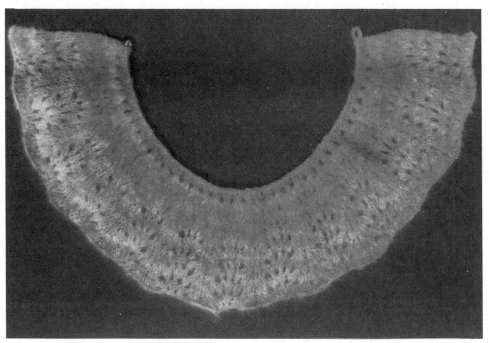

Harvesting cat hair is well worth the effort. This lace collar of cat hair was made by Louise O'Donnell. (Photo courtesy of *Shuttle, Spindle and Dyepot,* The Handweavers Guild of America, Lisa Clayton, photographer.)

the fuzz for a worthy cause makes this chore almost fun. (It's also a great way for a working woman to find out which cat sleeps where during the day.) Anne has collected an extraordinary amount of cat fuzz using this method, and boasts that her house is much cleaner than it ever was before she became obsessed with spinning pet fuzz.

Because cat hair tends to mat easily, you should avoid washing fuzz collected using the "housecleaning" method. Simply card it lightly and wash the yarn after spinning.

Sorting the Harvest

Whatever method you use to collect the fuzz, you should sort through it before storing it. You will obviously want to remove any burrs or other foreign matter and discard them. But you should also sort by color and texture.

If you have a double-coated pet, there will be both soft fuzzy fibers and coarser more hairlike fibers in your collection. We usually like to remove the guard hairs, because using the fuzzy fibers alone gives us a softer yarn.

Many pets also have different colors of fur, and we suggest that you

Two types of fibers from a handful of Newfoundland. The fibers on the left are the guard hairs, and the fibers on the right are the softer under-coat preferred for spinning.

keep the colors separate as you collect them. You can either spin several different colors from your pet—we have created some wonderful sweaters using stripes of different colors from the same dog—or combine the different colors when carding to make a heather-type yarn. You will be in a better position to make that decision when you have collected enough to spin, and it is obviously much easier to keep colors and textures separate while you are collecting than to go back and try to separate them later!

How to Store the Harvest

Keep the collected fur in a brown paper grocery bag sealed with tape, and store it in a cool, dark place. Don't pack the fuzz tightly or it may get matted. It is a good idea to make sure the bag is tightly sealed so that moths and other pests can't get at the fur. But check it a few days after sealing the bag to be sure that it isn't at all damp, because your fur can get real nasty if it mildews.

Dog hair seems to keep well for long periods of time. Kendall recently found a box in the attic that had remained unopened through two household moves. It contained brushings from her beautiful Golden Retriever, Abigail, who departed this life in 1986. Her legacy is now a scarf.

How Much Is Enough?

The length of time that it will take you to collect a sufficient quantity of fur to spin will vary radically. Obviously, it's quicker to get a sweater's worth from a Newfoundland than from a Toy Poodle. And your harvest will be affected not only by the size of your pet and the texture of his coat, but also by how often you brush him—and even by what time of year you begin collecting.

One of the first dogs Kendall spun was Ollie, a handsome Great

Pyrenees who lives with Kendall's friends Barbara and Jim in New York. Whenever they got together, Barb would give Kendall a little bag of Ollie fuzz. One day Kendall looked in the closet and decided it was time to spin some Ollie so she could make Barbara a scarf. She washed the fuzz, and spun it . . . and spun it and spun it. She was astounded at how much yarn those little bags of fuzz yielded. The result was not simply a scarf, but a sweater for Barbara and a vest for Jim!

The question of how much you need is really two questions:

1. How much yarn will I get from this pile of fuzz?

2. How much yarn will I need to make something from it?

This tam, modeled by Kendall's sister Cynthia, took less than four ounces of fuzz to make.

Both of these questions are difficult to answer with real precision, but we can give you some guidelines that will help you estimate.

Before you transform your pile of fuzz into yarn, the only way to "measure" it is to weigh it. Knowing how many ounces of raw fuzz you have will give you an indication of whether you're in the sweater ballpark or the hat ballpark, but to estimate more precisely what you can make, you should measure yardage after you spin your yarn. Weighing the fuzz—or the finished yarn—can't accurately tell you how many yards of yarn you have, because ever spinner spins differently. The yardage yield of raw fuzz or fleece depends on how thick the strand of yarn is. Four ounces of fuzz will produce more yards if the yarn is thin, and fewer yards if the yarn is thick.

Most beginning spinners will tend to spin thicker yarns, so you can assume that your first efforts will be in the "bulky" or perhaps the "worsted" range. You should strive for the thinnest possible yarn, however, because pet hair tends to be quite heavy, and you don't want to end up with a garment that is too warm to wear!

The simplest way to get a rough estimate of how much yarn is needed for a particular project is to look through knitting pattern books. The number of ounces and the yardage called for in the instructions will give you an idea of how big a project you can undertake.

Small projects, such as hats or mittens, require only a few ounces of yarn. The following chart shows the approximate yardage required to knit a sweater. The bulky yarn figures assume a gauge of 3½ to 4 stitches per inch. The worsted yarn figures assume a gauge of 4½ to 5 stitches per inch.

You may be delighted to find that you have enough yarn for the perfect sweater, but if not, don't be discouraged! Remember that you can combine your pet fibers with wool by blending them with wool when carding or by plying a strand of pet yarn with a strand of wool. Blending pet fuzz and wool will not only stretch your harvest, it will also give you a yarn with greater elasticity and "breathability."

You can also use your pet yarn in combination with store-bought yarn to make stripes or a picture. Check the projects in Chapter 8 for some ideas!

APPROXIMATE YARDAGE FOR SWEATERS

Size	Bulky Yarn (in yards)	Worsted Yarn (in yards)
Children's 4	500	500
Children's 4	600	600
Children's 4	650	700
Children's 4	800	800
Women's Small	900	950
Women's Medium	1000	1050
Women's Large	1100	1150
Men's Small	1100	1250
Men's Medium	1200	1450
Men's Large	1200	1250
Men's Extra Large	1400	1700

3

Preparing the Fuzz
for Spinning

Washing the Fuzz

When you tell your friends you're making a sweater from your pet, the very first thing they'll probably exclaim is "But won't you smell like a dog?" Well, the answer is no, not at all, if you take care to wash the fuzz carefully. Believe us—any kind of fleece can be washed to eliminate any conceivable odor. If you have ever been anywhere near wet sheep, you will know that they are significantly more fragrant than wet dogs, and most of us are not running around wearing "sheepish" sweaters.

Don't bother to wash the fuzz as you collect it. We recommend that you wait until you have a fairly substantial batch, because washing fuzz is something of a production. We can

assure you, however, that washing brushings is significantly easier than washing dog hair that is still attached to a squirming dog.

There are two schools of thought on when to wash—before spinning or after spinning. Many dog-hair spinners we interviewed spin right after sorting, without washing or carding the fuzz. They then wash the spun skeins of yarn.

We also found a large contingent who believe they get better results by washing before spinning (the washed fuzz must then be carded before spinning).

If your fuzz comes straight from your own fairly clean pet, you probably don't need to wash it first. But if it seems to be particularly dirty or smelly, you will find working with it to be a vastly more pleasant experience if it's clean.

A final caveat: if your fuzz has come from a kennel or a groomer, or has flea powder or grooming powder in it, you should wash it before spinning to remove any chemical residue. We heard from a woman who tried to spin her own dog's clippings after they had been swept off a groomer's floor. Something from the floor contaminated the pile of dog fuzz, and she had a nasty allergic reaction—and has never attempted to spin dog hair again.

The best place to wash your unspun fuzz is in the kitchen sink. Securely fasten a piece of cheesecloth or an old stocking over the drain to keep any stray dog hairs from clogging your plumbing. Spread an old towel on the counter next to the sink, and have a few more towels handy.

Fill the sink about three-quarters full with lukewarm water. The water temperature for washing sheep wool is absolutely critical, because water that is too hot, or that suddenly changes temperature, can cause the fibers to "felt" or mat together into an unspinnable mass. While some dog fibers seem quite felt-resistant, others are prone to matting and felting. Lukewarm water will get your fuzz perfectly clean, so you might as well use it and not worry about whether your breed will mat.

We have experimented with a variety of soaps and detergents, and have found that laundry detergent or dishwashing liquid—about a quarter of a cup to a sink—works quite well on pet hair. Some dog spinners insist on using only a very mild soap. But the best choice is your dog's shampoo, because most dog shampoos have special ingredients designed to eliminate odors. You can obtain a highly concentrated shampoo from a groomer, but the supermarket variety works fine. You'll need about half a cup of dog shampoo per sink. You can purchase a special dog shampoo designed for white coats at most pet stores or through a groomer—it does seem to brighten up the color.

Mix the detergent or dog shampoo in the water with your hands. Add your pet hair and stir it until it is fully submerged. Let it stand for five minutes (or longer, if you have other things to do) and drain the water, being careful not to dislodge the screen or stocking.

Fill the sink with lukewarm water again, add more detergent or dog shampoo, and stir the fibers with your hands. Repeat this process until the fibers are very clean—this can take up to four or five separate washings even if you don't keep a particularly dirty pet.

Drain the water and fill the sink with fresh lukewarm water, stirring the fibers to remove all traces of detergent. Drain and repeat *at least twice* to make sure the fibers are completely rinsed.

Drain the water again and let the fibers sit for a few minutes to drip. Lift the wet fuzz out, one handful at a time, gently squeezing the water out of each handful. Place the damp fuzz on a towel and repeat until all the fibers are out of the sink. Roll the towel up quite firmly to squeeze out more moisture.

Drying the Fuzz

Spread out several dry towels in a spot where they won't be in the way for a day or two. We suggest someplace indoors, as we once lost a whole sweater's worth of Keeshond to a sudden afternoon breeze. Fluff the damp fuzz slightly and spread it out evenly to help it dry more quickly.

Check the fuzz over the next day or two to see how it is drying. Rearrange the fibers to speed the drying process. It is very important that the fuzz not be stored until it is completely dry, or you run the risk of mildew—which will ruin it!

Once the fuzz is completely dry, you can store it in brown paper grocery bags sealed with tape—or you can continue to the next step, preparing it for spinning!

Oiling the Fuzz

If you have washed your fuzz, you will have removed most of the natural oil in the coat, and you should replace it by adding a small amount of oil to the fibers. The oil will make the fuzz easier to work with, and it combats static electricity to keep tiny particles of fuzz from floating free and tickling your nose.

You can use any kind of clear oil, such as baby oil or mineral oil. Some spinners use olive or vegetable oil, but these can go rancid if they are not completely washed out after spinning.

We like mineral oil because it is odorless, clear, and washes out easily. Make a mixture of three parts mineral oil and two parts water. Emulsify the mixture in the blender or food processor and pour it into a plastic spray bottle. Spread your clean fuzz on a towel and *lightly* spray the emulsion on the dog hair, mixing the fibers well to evenly disperse the oil. Wrap the fuzz in the towel overnight to let it fully and evenly absorb the oil. We don't recommend storing oiled fuzz too long, so plan to apply the oil no more than a day or two before carding and spinning.

Another method is to wait until after carding to add the oil. This works well for silky fibers that don't tend to fly around the room, but with fine pet fuzz, having the fibers oiled before carding helps keep the fibers from floating free. Using the same formula of emulsified oil and water, spray your fingers before you begin to spin, and keep them oiled as you work.

Carding

If you haven't washed your fuzz, you don't have to card the fibers before spinning, but if it has been washed, carding is a must. It makes the fibers easier to spin, and it gives you a nicer finished yarn. The washing process tends to make the fibers clump together and get a little tangled; carding separates the fibers, aligns them, and removes small tangles and any foreign matter that didn't come out in the wash.

You will also have to card if you are blending fibers. Fibers less than two inches long should be blended with longer fibers, from either an-

A pair of carders. They look remarkably similar to a dog slicker brush, but this set is slightly curved.

other dog breed or a sheep. Those of you who own short-haired breeds such as Beagles or Boxers must use the process we call "sprinkling," combining those short fibers with wool or longer dog fibers. Carding is the process that enables you to blend the fibers in preparation for spinning.

The principle behind carding is simply to line up all the fibers in parallel, much like brushing your hair. The tools for carding are called carding combs or carders—which is logical but curiously unimaginative for a craft that includes tools with names such as the niddy-noddy and the lazy kate. Carders are like a cross between a brush and a comb—they have hundreds of little wire bristles. In fact, they look very much like dog slicker brushes. You can purchase carders at a craft store or through the mail from one of the sources of spinning supplies listed in the back of this book. They come in various sizes—your store will be able to help you choose the most appropriate for your pet's

hair. We use a carder with fairly close-set teeth.

Your carders will work much more efficiently—and last much longer—if you designate a right-hand and a left-hand carder and always use the same one in the same hand. We put a rubber band around the right-hand carder, but you can also mark them "R" and "L." The following directions are for right-handed people. Some of our best friends are southpaws, and we realize that you are very adept at transposing instructions.

Sit comfortably with a towel or old sheet on your lap to catch wayward bits of fuzz. Before you begin carding, pick up a handful of clean fibers and gently tease them apart, separating the clumps that may have developed in washing. Put a few fuzz balls onto your left-hand carder—don't try

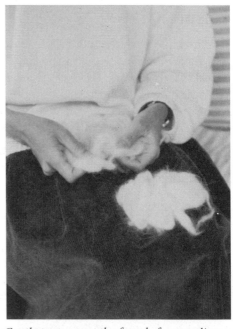

Gently tease apart the fuzz before carding.

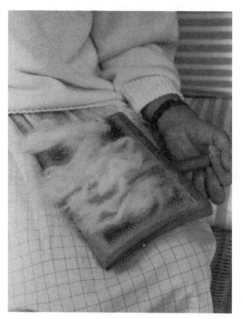

Put a few tufts of fibers on the left-hand carder.

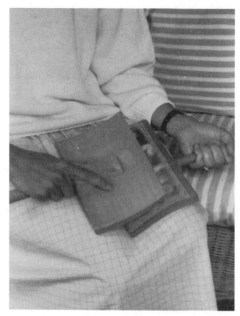

Draw the right-hand carder across the left-hand carder.

to put on too many or you won't be able to brush through all the fibers. If you are blending fibers, tease and mix them together a bit before putting them on the left-hand carder.

Hold the left-hand carder with the handle pointing away from you. Hold the right-hand carder with the handle pointing back toward you and lightly draw it down over the left-hand carder. Repeat two or three times. There will be less resistance on the second and subsequent passes than on the first pass, as the fibers align themselves in the teeth.

Most of the fibers will be aligned in the left-hand carder. Some of the fibers will have moved to the right-hand one, and you'll need to move them back. Turn the right-hand carder around so its handle is also point-

Most of the fibers are aligned in the left-hand carder.

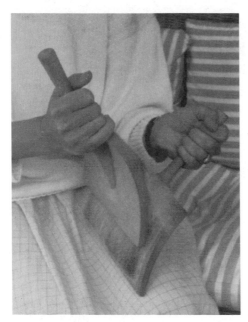

Draw the right-hand carder up across the left-hand carder to transfer the fibers back to the left-hand carder.

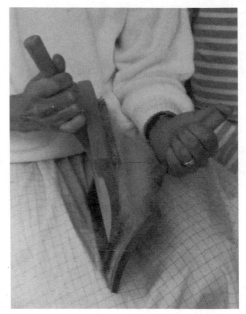

Brush the bottom of the right-hand carder down against the top of the left-hand carder to release the fibers.

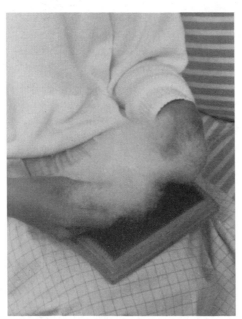

Pull the pillow of carded fibers off the carder.

Roll the fibers into a sausage-shaped rolag.

ing away from you. Pull it up across the left-hand one—against the grain—to release its fuzz. (This is a lot like getting the lint out of the lint brush once you have the lint off your clothes.)

Repeat these steps until the fibers are all aligned in the teeth of the left-hand carder. If you are blending, continue until the fibers are evenly blended together. To remove the fibers from the carder, turn the right-hand one around again, so that both of the handles point away from you, and gently brush the bottom of the right-hand carder against the top of the left-hand one to push the fibers out of the teeth. You will have a roughly rectangular pillow of fibers, which should be rolled into a sausage shape. This sausage is called a rolag, and the rolag is the material that you are going to spin.

Kendall, Meg, and Martha working together on the front porch. Meg is learning to card, and Martha says she's "helping."

Blending Fibers

If you are blending fibers—dog with wool, short-haired dog with long-haired dog, "sprinkles" with longer fibers, or different colors—begin by arranging alternate fibers on the left-hand carder. Card as outlined above until the fibers are evenly blended—this may require a few more passes.

Before You Spin

We suggest that you make a good supply of rolags before you start to spin. Once you get into the rhythm of spinning, it can be frustrating to have to stop and make more rolags.

Better yet, enlist a friend, spouse, or child to do your carding for you. It's really much simpler to do than it is to explain, and once you've got the hang of it, it will be easy to teach someone else. Carding the fuzz and making rolags can keep your family occupied while you do the spinning—it's a great way to get the whole family involved in your pet-hair project!

We like to keep our rolags in a basket until we're ready to spin. Don't cram them in tightly—they should be placed gently in the basket so they don't get matted or stuck together.

Spinning the Yarn

Spinning is quite simply the process of transforming a lot of short fibers into one long strand of yarn. The two actions necessary to accomplish this are twisting the fibers together as you are drawing or pulling them out. As you twist a length of fibers, the next group of fibers slightly overlaps to bond the shorter lengths into a continuous strand.

By far the easiest way to learn how to spin is to sit next to someone who's doing it. Spinning is more popular than you might have expected, and classes and demonstrations are given all across the country. If you would like to find a spinner in your area, you can contact the Handweavers Guild of America, Inc., 2402 University Avenue, Suite 702, Minneapolis, MN 55114; (612) 646-0802.

It is, of course, also possible to learn to spin from a book, and that is precisely what we plan to *help* you do here in this chapter. Even if you find a spinning teacher, it's worth reading this to get a bit of a head start.

If, however, you have no desire to learn to spin (the idea gives Anne hives), simply refer to the list of seasoned spinners, who are willing to do the spinning for you, at the end of this book.

Now, we have to come out and admit right here that it is a little bit easier to learn to spin sheep wool than pet fuzz. Pet fuzz is quite slippery and fine, while sheep wool has a natural twist to it, is quite elastic, and is naturally lubricated with lanolin, all of which help its "spinability." Come to think of it, that's

Thomas Crolius (Kendall's father) made this drop spindle from scrap lumber. It works just as well as the store-bought one.

probably why our ancestors were tending flocks of sheep instead of flocks of dogs and cats. It sure wasn't because the sheep were smart or affectionate or particularly companionable.

Take a hint from the shepherds, though, and start to learn spinning with wool. You can buy a few ounces of clean, carded wool from your craft store or by mail from one of the sources listed in this book.

You can move up to dog hair quite quickly with a method used by Jerie Lucas, possibly the foremost dog-hair spinning expert in the country. Jerie has her students prepare three rolags: one that is 50 percent wool and 50 percent dog hair, a second that is 25 percent wool and 75 percent dog hair, and the third of 100 percent dog hair. As Jerie notes, it takes only three rolags to learn!

Spinning on a Drop Spindle

You can buy a drop spindle from your crafts store or you can make one yourself using the directions on page 23. A drop spindle looks like an elongated child's top with a disk—called a whorl—at the bottom of a long, notched shaft.

To begin spinning on a drop spindle, tie a twenty-four-inch length of store-bought yarn to the shaft just above the whorl. Wrap it around the bottom of the shaft a few times, and then wrap it up the shaft to the notch and hook the yarn into the notch firmly. If it seems to slip, you can use a half hitch at the notch to keep the yarn secure.

Stand or sit on a high stool so the spindle can move freely. Hold your fibers for spinning in your left hand. Draw out a pinch of fibers and overlap them about three inches with the end of the store-bought yarn. With your right hand, give the spindle a sharp clockwise turn. As the spindle is turning, grasp the fibers with your right hand at the point of overlap and move your left hand a few inches up the fibers. Release your right hand and let the twist run up to your left hand. The fibers will now be joined to the store-bought yarn.

With your left hand, pinch the yarn at the point where it joins the fibers and give the spindle another clockwise turn with your right hand. Move your right hand back to pinch

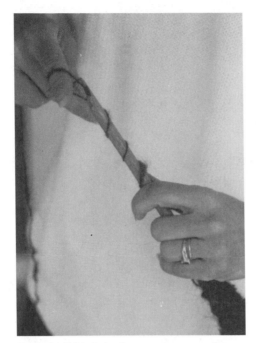

Put a half-hitch in the yarn to secure it to the hook at the top of the spindle.

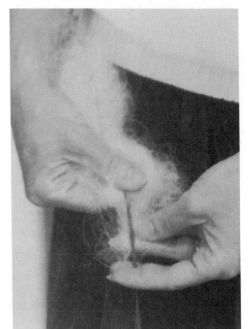

Overlap a section of unspun fibers with the last three inches of the leader yarn.

the yarn just below your left hand, and draw out another two to three inches of fibers with your left hand. Release your right hand and let the twist run up the fibers to your left hand.

Repeat these steps:

1. Pinch with the left hand and turn the spindle with the right.

2. Pinch with the right hand and draw out fibers with the left.

3. Pinch with the left hand and release the right.

When you have spun about twenty-four to thirty inches of yarn, wind it evenly onto the spindle shaft in a cone shape and hook it through the notch at the top of the shaft, or tie another half hitch, leaving about eight

Spin the spindle clockwise with your left hand.

to ten inches of spun yarn above the notch. Proceed with spinning and winding the yarn onto the spindle until the spindle is full. You can slip the cone of yarn gently off the top of the shaft and keep it in that form until you are ready to skein it.

Helpful Hints for Using a Drop Spindle

Ideally, you should be spinning yarn of a consistent thickness and with a consistent amount of twist, but this comes with practice. While pet hair is best when spun quite fine, don't try to spin too fine a yarn when you're first learning. The finer the yarn, the more twist is required to keep it from breaking, and this can be difficult to achieve at first.

Be sure that the spindle is always turning in a clockwise direction. If you reverse its direction, you will "unspin" the yarn you have spun and it will break.

If your yarn breaks, and it most certainly will as you are learning to spin, give the yarn more twist before drawing out more fibers. It may be helpful to let the spindle rest on the floor while it is spinning. That will reduce the pull on the yarn, though it doesn't allow the spindle to spin as freely.

When your yarn breaks, or when you need to add a new bunch of fibers, simply overlap about three-inches of the unspun fibers with the spun end of yarn as you did when you first attached the fibers to the store-bought yarn you used as a leader.

If your yarn is very kinky and twists back on itself, you have given it too much twist. Try spinning the spindle a bit slower and drawing out more fibers.

Above all, try not to get frustrated. Every beginning spinner faces a point where he or she thinks this can't possibly be done without having an extra hand or two. Luckily, this point usually comes just before the moment of revelation, when all of the confusing hand motions just seem to click and you "get it." Don't give up!

Don't worry if your yarn looks sort of lumpy and bumpy—that's what every spinner's first efforts look like! With practice, you will soon be spinning gorgeous yarn. However, this is another good reason to learn to spin with sheep wool—you may just want to throw out the first yarn you spin—and you want to be perfectly comfortable with spinning before you tackle that precious dog fuzz!

Making a Drop Spindle

MATERIALS NEEDED

3" circle cut from scrap 1" lumber (the handyman in your household may point out that 1" lumber is actually only $\frac{3}{4}$" thick—we know that, and it's fine)

12" length of $\frac{1}{4}$" or $\frac{3}{8}$" dowel

Fine and coarse sandpaper

Glue

Mark the exact center of the circle of wood and drill a 1/4" or 3/8" hole, depending on the size of dowel used. Cut a slanted notch about 1" from one end of the dowel, as indicated in the illustration. Taper the other end

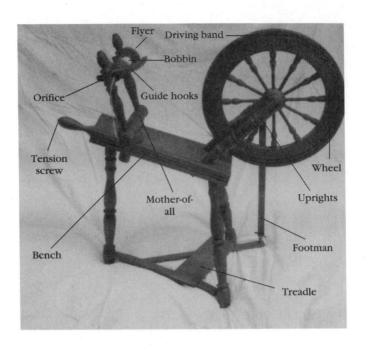

Flyer   Driving band

Bobbin

Orifice   Guide hooks

Tension screw

Wheel

Mother-of-all

Uprights

Bench

Footman

Treadle

of the dowel, somewhat like a top. Sand all surfaces of the disk and dowel, including the area in the notch, until they are smooth. It is important to get all the surfaces completely smooth so that your yarn won't snag on a rough spot.

Insert the dowel into the hole so that the tapered end extends about 1½" to 2". Glue in place.

About Spinning Wheels

While a spinning wheel is faster, easier, and more efficient than a drop spindle, it does require a pretty significant investment. If you get hooked on spinning you'll probably want to make that investment. Some craft stores will rent spinning wheels, and that can be a terrific way to help you decide if you want to purchase one—it's also a terrific, inexpensive

way to get your dog fuzz spun for your first project.

We don't recommend buying an old spinning wheel at an antiques store or flea market until you really know what you're looking for. Many old wheels lack essential parts that you might not realize are missing. Some old wheels are badly warped and will just never work well.

The most popular kind of wheel is a treadle wheel. There are several types of treadle wheels, and they are available in both traditional and modern designs. Your local craft store, or one of the suppliers listed in the appendix, can give you more information about different types.

Spinning on a Treadle Wheel

Before you begin spinning on a wheel, you should be familiar with the differ-

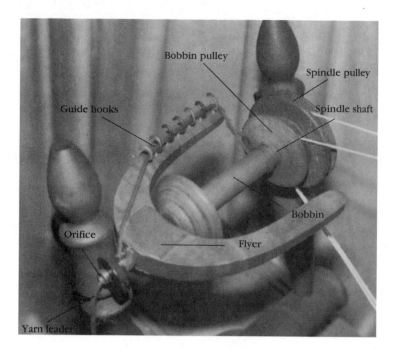

Bobbin pulley

Spindle pulley

Spindle shaft

Guide hooks

Bobbin

Orifice

Flyer

Yarn leader

ent parts of the wheel and their specific functions. Since spinning requires you to perform several tasks simultaneously, it helps to practice each individually before you begin. The first step is to practice treadling without spinning. Sit at the wheel and put your foot on the treadle. You should wear flat shoes—or no shoes—not heels. Give the wheel a clockwise push to get it going, and push the treadle using a "heel-to-toe" action.

The idea is to treadle evenly to keep the wheel turning evenly. It's not a race—the wheel should not be going too fast, but if you slow down too much, the wheel has a tendency to stop and reverse direction. It is very important to keep the wheel turning in a clockwise direction. Once you begin to spin, your hands are going to be very busy, so it's worth the time to practice treadling

until it becomes second nature. You can test your proficiency by letting the wheel stop and then getting it going again in a clockwise direction without using your hands.

When your foot has mastered its role in the process, you can begin to spin. Tie an eighteen-to-twenty-four-inch length of store-bought yarn to the bobbin. First, pass it over the guide hook closest to you. Put a crochet hook through the orifice and draw the yarn out through the orifice. Wind the leader yarn onto the bobbin by turning the wheel clockwise until about eight inches protrude from the orifice. Overlap the fibers of the rolag on the last three inches of the leader yarn. Holding the yarn with your left hand at the point of the join, give the wheel a push with your right hand and begin treadling slowly. Draw out some fibers with

Thread the yarn through the guide hooks and through the orifice with the help of a crochet hook.

Pinch the yarn with your left hand while drawing out fibers with your right hand. When you release your left hand the twist will run up your right hand.

Let the wheel pull the spun yarn onto the bobbin.

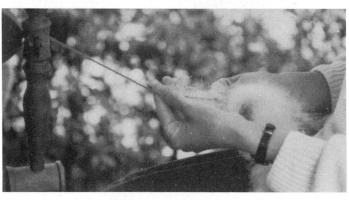

Attach a new rolag by overlapping the fibers with the end of your spun yarn.

your right hand and release your left hand to allow the twist to run up the drafted fibers. Keep the yarn taut, but don't pull on it too hard. Move your left hand back to just in front of your right hand and pinch. Draw out more fibers with your right hand and release your left hand.

When you have spun a length of yarn, keep your right hand "pinched" on the yarn but let your hand be pulled toward the orifice. The action of the wheel will draw the spun yarn onto the bobbin. As you practice, these motions of spinning the yarn and allowing it to be drawn onto the spindle will become one continuous, fluid motion, but as you are learning, it is simpler to think of them as separate motions.

When you finish a rolag, move the yarn to the next guide hook and attach a new rolag by overlapping it with the spun end of your yarn. Continue to spin and move up and back down the guide hooks until the bobbin is full.

Helpful Hints for Using a Spinning Wheel

If your yarn breaks and disappears through the orifice, try giving the yarn more twist before you let it wind onto the bobbin. This is bound to happen while you're learning, so keep that crochet hook close by to pull the spun end of the yarn back

out through the orifice. Overlap the fibers of the rolag with the spun yarn and begin again.

If your yarn kinks up when you release it to be wound on the bobbin, you need less twist in the yarn. Try treadling more slowly than you have been.

If the yarn won't wind onto the bobbin, see if it is caught on the guide hook. Make sure the yarn you are spinning isn't too thick to pass through the orifice easily. You can also tighten the tension of the drive band slightly to pull the yarn on faster. It is often necessary to tighten the drive band as the bobbin fills and becomes heavier.

For Experienced Spinners

All of the pet-hair spinning experts we consulted agree that the best way to spin dog or cat hair is quite fine, and with a lot of twist. Pet fibers are not as elastic as wool and can be very heavy, so a finer yarn—particularly when blended or plied with wool—gives the best result. Soft fibers from the undercoat should be spun with the woolen method, while longer, hairlike fibers can also be spun worsted. A tight twist will ensure a durable yarn and will minimize—though not completely prevent—the shedding typical of this type of fiber.

5

Finishing the Yarn

After you have spun your yarn, there are several more steps to take before it is ready to use. Even if you washed the fuzz before spinning, hand-spun yarn must be washed again to remove the oil added to it and to set the twist. You may also want to ply the yarn before using it.

Plying the Yarn

Plying yarn is simply twisting two or more strands into a thicker strand. Most knitting yarns are two-ply, although you can certainly knit with a one-ply yarn. Plying is a matter of personal preference, but it has several advantages. First, it makes a stronger yarn and helps to compensate for any weak spots in your single strands—a real plus for beginning

spinners. It also helps to "relax" yarns that are overtwisted and kinky, because plying is done with a twist that is opposite to the one used to spin the individual strands.

You can ply strands of the same yarn or combine different types of yarn—we have plied two types of dog yarn, and even dog yarn with cat yarn. Many dog-hair spinners recommend plying a strand of dog yarn with a strand of wool. Dog yarn is very warm, tends to hold moisture in, and is less elastic than wool. A combination of dog and wool gives you yarn that is warm but not too hot, "breathes" better, and is more elastic than dog yarn alone, with the fuzzy texture and softness you can't get from only wool—truly the best of both worlds. You will get the best

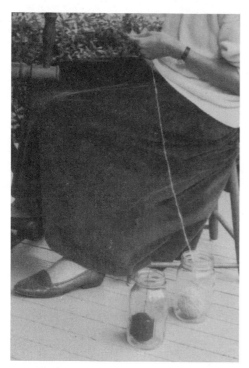

Putting the balls of yarn to be plied in jars will keep them from tangling as they unwind.

without getting tangled in each other. There is a special tool called a lazy kate that holds bobbins of yarn, but you can get very satisfactory results by simply putting two balls of yarn in two jars on the floor.

Plying on a Drop Spindle

Attach a leader of store-bought yarn, about eighteen inches long, to the spindle. Tie the two ends of your balls or bobbins of spun yarn to the leader yarn. Hold the yarn in your left hand, with one strand of yarn on either side of your middle finger.

With your right hand, spin the spindle counterclockwise. Let the strands pass through your fingers as

results if the yarns you ply are of equal thickness.

The twist in yarn is described as either a "Z twist" or an "S twist," depending on the direction in which the drop spindle or the spinning wheel is turned to spin the yarn. The spinning directions in this book are all for "Z twist" yarns, formed by turning the spindle or the wheel in a clockwise direction. "Z twist" yarns should be plied with an "S twist." You can use a drop spindle or a wheel to ply your yarn.

To prepare for plying, you'll need two bobbins, cones, or loosely wound balls of your spun yarn. They will need to be able to unwind easily

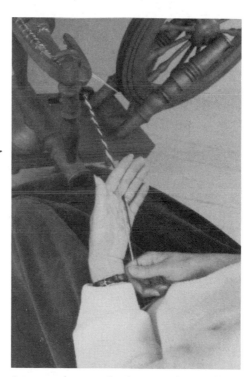

Separate the strands of yarn with your fingers while plying.

they twist together. When the drop spindle reaches the floor, wind the plied yarn onto the shaft in a cone shape as you did when you were spinning.

Plying on a Spinning Wheel

Attach a leader of store-bought yarn to the bobbin and tie the two ends of your balls or bobbins of spun yarn to the leader. Wind the leader yarn onto the bobbin until the knot of the hand-spun yarn passes through the orifice and past the guide hook.

Hold the yarn in your left hand, with one strand of yarn on either side of your middle finger. With your right hand, turn the wheel counterclockwise and begin treadling. Let the yarn pass through your fingers evenly, and allow it to be drawn up onto the bobbin.

Skeining Your Yarn

Whether you are using single-ply or plied yarn, the yarn must be made into skeins before washing to set the twist. Winding the yarn into skeins also allows you to count the yardage so that you can plan your project.

Winding yarn into skeins can be accomplished using specific tools designed for skeining, such as a swift or the delightfully named niddy-noddy, but you can easily improvise your own skeining tool.

Cut a stiff piece of cardboard about eighteen to twenty-four inches long and cover the rough edges with masking tape so the yarn won't catch on them. Wind your yarn around the cardboard. Using white yarn (colored yarn can run and streak your hand-

This contraption is called a niddy-noddy, and it is very useful for making uniform skeins. You can also use a coat hanger or a piece of cardboard.

spun yarn), tie the wound yarn in three or four places to form a skein, and slip it off the cardboard.

Setting the Twist

When you remove your skeins from your yarn winder, you may notice a lot of kinks in the yarn. These can be eased out by washing the yarn. You'll need to wash the yarn anyway to remove all traces of the oil you added before spinning it.

Dissolve a few tablespoons of dog shampoo or detergent in a sink of lukewarm water. Place a few skeins

Golden Retriever, Great Pyrenees, and Newfoundland skeins drying on the back porch. The rolling pin works well as a weight.

in the sink and let them soak for several minutes. Drain the sink and fill with fresh lukewarm water. If you did not wash your fuzz before spinning, you will need to repeat the washing several times. When the yarn is completely clean, fill the sink with lukewarm water to rinse. Repeat the rinse process until all traces of detergent are gone.

Let the water drain from the sink and lift the skeins out, gently squeezing them to remove the water.

If you plan to dye your yarn, this is the point at which you should do it. Skip to Chapter 6: "Dyeing Your

Pet Yarn." Be sure that the yarn tying the skeins isn't too tight—if it is too tight, the dye will not be able to penetrate the yarn evenly.

Loop the skeins over a clean dowel or broom handle. Hang a small weight through the bottom of the skeins to keep the yarn straight as it dries. When the skeins are dry, slip them off the dowel or broom handle.

Measuring Yardage

After you have given your skeins their final wash and let them dry, you should measure the yardage. Measure the length of one revolution of the skein without stretching the skein too much. Count the number of threads in each skein, and multiply by the length of the revolution. Divide the number by thirty-six to arrive at the number of yards in the skein.

EXAMPLE

Length of one revolution: 52"

Number of threads in the skein: 38

52" x 38 = 1,976"

1,976" ÷ 36 = 54.88, or about 54¾ yards

Label each skein with its yardage. We use the small cardboard tags with strings. You can also add any other pertinent information to the tag, like breed of dog, the date, and so on.

Twisting the Skeins

Put your hands through the two ends of the skein and twist it. Fold the skein over and twist again, then tuck one end of the skein into the other end.

As pretty as your homespun skeins are, you shouldn't keep them on display too long. Store the skeins in a paper bag sealed with tape to keep moths and other pests away from them. Wind them into balls before using them for knitting or other projects.

A basketful of dog yarn: Golden Retriever, Collie, Samoyed, Lhasa Apso, and Shih Tzu.

Dyeing Your Pet Yarn

One of the most appealing aspects of creating projects from pet yarn is having a finished product that is reminiscent of your beloved pet.

This is especially true if you are hoping to create a keepsake from your companion's coat (Anne is still really upset that she doesn't have any fuzz from her late Bouvier, Irish). But it's a wonderful tribute to your live pet, too—after all, strolling down the avenue sporting a scarf or sweater that exactly matches your pooch's pelt does give one a certain cachet.

Besides, pet hair comes in such wonderful, natural colors. What could be more lovely than a richly colored Golden Retriever scarf setting off your camel's hair coat? What could be prettier than the soft, white glow of a Samoyed sweater, or more handsome than the gray-black tones of a Poodle vest?

However, if you are determined to dye this naturally beautiful material, it certainly can be done. You can use store-bought dyes or experiment with natural ones, such as marigold petals and onion skins. Even Kool-Aid has its proponents as an inexpensive and nontoxic dyestuff.

Yarn can be dyed either before or after spinning. You've heard the expression "dyed in the wool"? Well, that comes from dyeing the fibers before they are spun. If you dye before you spin, be sure to wash your fuzz first.

If you dye the yarn after it is spun, it should be in skeins, not in balls, so the dye can penetrate the fibers easily and evenly. The skeins should be loosely tied so you don't end up with a tie-dyed effect. And because the skeins should be wet before you put them in the dyebath, most spinners dye them right after they're washed.

There are many books on how to dye yarn in your library or your craft store. Since we do not quite approve of this business of dyeing pet yarn, we won't encourage it by including instructions here—you're on your own!

We will tell you that pet fuzz accepts color just as well as sheep wool, though the coarser guard hairs do not accept color well. Colors always look darker when the yarn is wet, so keep this in mind when you're deciding when to remove your skeins from the dyebath. In any case, dyeing any kind of yarn always involves quite a bit of experimentation, so we suggest that you test a smallish sample before dunking all your precious pet yarn.

7

Making Things from Your Pet Yarn

Pet yarn can be used in place of sheep wool for any of your favorite crafts—knitting, crochet, needlepoint, embroidery, weaving, and so forth. You can use your favorite patterns, create your own patterns, or try one of the projects included in this book.

There are a few tips you should keep in mind when using pet yarn instead of store-bought yarns.

Knitting

Pet yarn knits up beautifully. The only difference between using your pet yarn and store-bought yarn is that you will have to be particularly careful to check your knitting gauge.

Any hand-spun yarn, whether from a sheep or a dog, is likely to be a bit less consistent in its thickness than a store-bought yarn. Knit a swatch approximately four inches by four inches and measure how many stitches per inch it yields. Change to a smaller or larger pair of needles and knit another four-inch-square swatch until you achieve the desired gauge.

We also suggest that you knit swatches from at least two balls of your yarn. Your first spinning efforts may tend to be a little erratic, and checking swatches from the first and last ball of yarn you spun will show you whether the difference is enough to affect your gauge.

Dog yarn can even be made into baskets. Diane Mortensen of Vancouver, B.C., created this from Keeshond, Samoyed, and a Shepherd-Collie cross, on a base of sea grass. (Photo courtesy of Diane Mortensen.)

Crochet

As with knitting, the key to success when crocheting with pet yarn is to check your gauge even more carefully than you ordinarily would. Again, this has less to do with the fact that it is pet yarn than with the fact that it is hand-spun and the thickness of the fiber may not be consistent, especially if you are a novice spinner.

Needlepoint and Embroidery

We have used pet yarn to do needlepoint, cross-stitch, and crewel embroidery. It is best to use a two-ply strand for the added strength it gives the yarn. This does require that you spin a very fine yarn, however, so that the plied yarn doesn't end up being too thick.

If you feel that your yarn may be a little more fragile than the embroidery wool you are accustomed to using, try embroidering with a slightly shorter strand of yarn than you would ordinarily use. While crewel work and cross-stitch usually are not too tough on the yarn, the friction of drawing the yarn through needlepoint canvas can sometimes fray it. Again, we suggest using a shorter length of yarn than you usually use, allowing you to make fewer passes through the canvas. Obviously, the fewer times you pull the yarn through the canvas, the easier it is on the yarn.

Weaving

The first pet yarn project we undertook was a lovely scarf woven from Golden Retriever yarn. A simple project like a scarf can be undertaken on a child's loom, and the process is so simple that, yes, even a child can do it.

Weaving involves two sets of yarns. The "warp" is the yarn that is placed on the loom to create the lengthwise fibers. The yarn that is woven in width-wise is called the "weft" or the "woof."

We recommend using store-bought wool as the warp, because it must be very strong so that it doesn't break when drawn taut on the loom. It should also be as smooth and abrasion resistant as possible to allow the width-wise yarns to move easily along the warp. So use store-bought yarn for the warp and save your pet hair to use for the woof. Now that's certainly easy to remember!

8

Projects

We've provided instructions for several projects you might like to try with your pet yarn. We're grateful to the spinners and knitters across the country who have shared their creations with us.

We realize that you probably just can't wait to make something, so we have focused on small projects such as mittens and hats, and we've included some very special sweater patterns for inspiration.

If you don't have very much pet yarn to work with, remember that you can use your pet yarn in combination with wool. Use it to make stripes in a sweater or in a pair of mittens. Or use it to knit a picture of your dog into a wool sweater. We've included designs for several breeds of dogs that you can use with one of

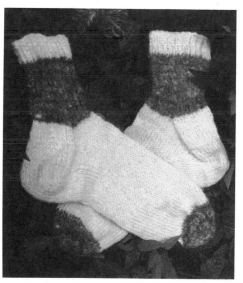

Even small amounts of pet yarn can be put to good use. Karen Agee made these skating socks, with heels and toes of soft cat yarn, for her daughter. (Photo courtesy of Karen Agee.)

our patterns or with your own favorite sweater pattern.

A caution: if you combine store-bought wool with your yarn, you will need to choose one that is as close as possible to the same thickness as the yarn you have spun. If your dog yarn is thinner than your store-bought yarn, the stitches will be smaller than the store-bought yarn stitches, so the stripes or design will alter the shape of the finished garment.

We have used standard knitting abbreviations in our patterns. For your reference, here they are:

K	knit
P	purl
st(s)	stitch(es)
inc	increase
dec	decrease

rem	remaining
sl	slip st
PSSO	pass slipped st over
BO	bind off
CO	cast on
beg	beginning
st st	stockinette stitch (K 1 row, P 1 row)
garter st	(K every row)
K2tog	knit 2 stitches together
P2tog	purl 2 stitches together
YO	yarn over
YF	with yarn in front
K1-B	insert needle in back of st and K1
P1-B	insert needle in back of st and P1

Golden Retriever Scarf

Scarves are a terrific project for pet-spun yarn. They are easy to make, don't require a lot of yarn, and because fit is not an issue, they are quite forgiving about uneven thicknesses of yarn—thus a great way to use your first petspun, which may be a bit inconsistent!

This scarf was made from Kendall's beloved Abigail. Abby was a red Golden Retriever—the hue of an Irish Setter—and the color is exquisite. The yarn is two-ply, and the scarf is knit in Seed Stitch on large needles for a lacy effect. Although it is light, it is very warm, and it looks beautiful with a camel hair coat.

Materials

Yarn: 3 ounces sport weight; approximately 150 yards

1 pair straight needles, size 10

Gauge: 3 stitches per inch in seed stitch (but with a scarf, gauge is not critical)

Instructions

Cast on 24 stitches loosely. Work in Seed Stitch throughout.
Row 1: *K1, P1; repeat across.
Row 2: *P1, K1; repeat across.

When the scarf measures 52 inches, or the desired length, or you're about to run out of yarn, bind off loosely.

Note that you're always knitting the purl stitches and purling the knit stitches. If you were to knit the knit stitches and purl the purl stitches,

This 100-percent Golden Retriever scarf is the perfect color to wear with a camel hair coat.

you'd end up with a ribbed scarf—which is also fine, but not what we did for this scarf.

Watch Cap

This cap is quick to knit and takes only about 200 yards of yarn to complete. It is knit quite tightly so it's delightfully warm, and the texture is just beautiful. Kendall's mother knit this from two-ply Newfoundland and two-ply Golden Retriever. The Newf yarn is so soft and glossy that if it weren't for the Golden Retriever pattern, you could easily mistake this for mink!

Materials

Yarn: 6 ounces worsted weight, approximately 170 yards main color; 35 yards pattern color

1 pair round needles and/or double-pointed needles, size 3 (or size required for gauge)

Gauge: 5 stitches per inch

This watch cap, designed by Patricia Crolius, is knit from Newfoundland and Golden Retriever.

Read diagrams from right to left, and repeat the pattern around the row. When working with two colors of yarn, carry the second yarn loosely in back, and twist the yarn in use around the yarn you carry every three stitches.

← Start here

Instructions

Cast on 120 stitches. Work in K2, P2 ribbing for 6 inches.

Knit one round.

Start pattern (see charts). Work 23 rounds in pattern for Fair Isle, or 26 rows for Hearts and Scotties.

At end of pattern, knit 1 round loosely (if using round needles, change to double-pointed needles here).

1st decrease round: *K2tog around (60 sts remaining).

2nd decrease round: *P2tog around (30 sts remaining).

3rd decrease round: *K2tog around (15 sts remaining).

4th decrease round: *P2tog to last 3 sts; P3tog.

Break yarn leaving an 8-inch strand. Run yarn through the remaining stitches twice. Pull together and secure on underside of cap.

Start here →

Meg's Tam

Kendall made this tam for Meg Charlton from finely spun yarn from Meg's Great Pyrenees, Ollie. We cannot describe how adorable the two of them look strolling to school together in Greenwich Village each morning. Using a blend of dog and wool yarn will give the tam greater elasticity and "body."

Size

One size fits all

Materials

Yarn: 1¾ ounces sport weight yarn

Straight needles size 6 and 8 (or size required for gauge)

Gauge: 5 stitches per inch in stockinette stitch, with larger needles

Instructions

With smaller needles, cast on 100 sts. Work K1, P1 ribbing for 4 rows.

Change to larger needles.

Note: Work all increases (see below) by knitting into front and back of st.

INCREASES:

Row 1: *Inc 1, K9; repeat across.
Row 2: Purl.
Row 3: *Inc 1, K10; repeat across.
Rows 4, 6, 8, 10: Purl.
Row 5: *Inc 1, K11; repeat across.
Row 7: *Inc 1, K12; repeat across.
Row 9: *Inc 1, K13; repeat across.

Meg Charlton models her favorite hat, a tam made from her beloved Great Pyrenees, Ollie.

Row 11: *Inc 1, K14; repeat across (160 sts on needle).
Rows 12–16: Work even in st st.

DECREASES:

Row 1: *K2tog, K28, K2tog; repeat across.
All even numbered rows: Purl.
Row 3: *K2tog, K26, K2tog; repeat across.
Row 5: *K2tog, K24, K2tog; repeat across.
Row 7: *K2tog, K22, K2tog; repeat across.
Row 9: *K2tog, K20, K2tog; repeat across.
Row 11: *K2tog, K18, K2tog; repeat across.
Row 13: *K2tog, K16, K2tog; repeat across.

Row 15: *K2tog, K14, K2tog; repeat across.

Row 17: *K2tog, K12, K2tog; repeat across.

Row 19: *K2tog, K10, K2tog; repeat across.

Row 21: *K2tog, K8, K2tog; repeat across.

Row 23: *K2tog, K6, K2tog; repeat across.

Row 25: *K2tog, K4, K2tog; repeat across.

Row 27: *K2tog, K2, K2tog; repeat across.

Row 29: *K2tog; repeat across.

Row 30: Purl rem 10 sts.

FINISHING:

Cut yarn, leaving a 20-inch length to sew with. Draw yarn through the remaining sts and fasten tightly. Sew seam.

Pill Box Hat of Cat Hair

Louise O'Donnell adapted a design from a commercial pattern to create this beautiful hat. Louise is a cat hair expert—in fact, she is the only master spinner in the United States with a Certificate of Excellence in cat hair!

Our thanks to Louise for sharing this with us, and for her expert advice on working with cat hair.

Size

One size fits all

Materials

Yarn: Approximately 2 to 3 ounces sport weight yarn

Straight needles, size 5 and 7

Gauge: 6 stitches per inch

Instructions

PATTERN: TWISTED RIB

Row 1: *K1-b, P1; repeat across.
Row 2: *K1, P1-b; repeat across.

PATTERN: OBLIQUE OPEN WORK

Row 1: K1, *YF, K2tog; end K1.
Row 2: Purl across.
Row 3: K2, *YF, K2tog; end K1.
Row 4: Purl across.

With smaller needles, cast on 76 sts. Work in Twisted Rib for 1 inch.

Change to larger needles and work reverse stockinette (purl side to right side of fabric) for 2 rows, ending with a purl row. Begin Oblique Open Work pattern and work the four pattern rows 5 times.

The hat and scarf, created by Louise O'Donnell, are both of cat yarn. (Photo courtesy of *Shuttle, Spindle and Dyepot,* The Handweavers Guild of America, Lisa Clayton, photographer.)

Next row: *K2, K2tog; repeat across, ending K4 (58 sts).
Next row: *K2, K2tog; repeat across, ending K2 (44 sts).

Continue in reverse stockinette for 1 inch.

Next row: *K2, K2tog; repeat across (22 sts).
Next row: Purl across.
Next row: *K2, K2tog; repeat across (11 sts).
Next row: Purl across.
Next row: *K2, K2tog; repeat across (6 sts).

Break yarn. Place rem sts on large bodkin. Thread yarn through last 6 sts, pull tight and sew side seam.

BLOCKING:

Wet thoroughly, squeeze out excess water, and place over a small bowl to dry.

Martha's Mittens

Kendall made these fluffy mittens for her daughter Martha. The yarn is Samoyed puppy singles plied with wool, and we had just enough of this special yarn to make these little mittens. Martha thinks it is just terrific that her mittens are made from puppy fur!

This basic pattern is a great place to start, but you can get very creative with mittens. Try initials, a Fair Isle pattern, or stripes of cat yarn alternating with dog yarn!

Sizes

Child's Small 2–4 (Medium 6–8 and Large 8–10)

Materials

Yarn: 1 (1½-2) ounces fingering yarn

Double-pointed needles, sizes 3 and 5 (or size required for gauge)

Gauge: 22 sts and 30 rows per 4 inches in stockinette stitch, with larger needles

Instructions

On smaller needles, cast on 34 (38-40) sts on three needles. Work in K1, P1 ribbing for 2 inches. Change to larger needles and work in st st for 8 (10-12) rounds.

Slip 1st 6 (7-7) sts onto holder for thumb. Cast on 6 (7-7) sts and continue working in st st until mitten measures 5½ (7-8) inches from cuff.

[For left mitten: K11 (12-13), put

Martha's mittens of Samoyed puppy are so soft she can't keep them off her face.

next 6 (7-7) sts on holder, CO 6 (7-7), and continue around.]

1st decrease row: K2tog, K13 (15-16), K2tog, K2tog, K13 (15-16), K2tog.

2nd decrease row: K2tog, K11 (13-14), K2tog, K2tog, K11 (13-14), K2tog.

3rd decrease row: K2tog, K9 (11-12), K2tog, K2tog, K9 (11-12), K2tog.

4th decrease row: K2tog, K7 (9-10), K2tog, K2tog, K7 (9-10), K2tog.

BO rem 18 (22-24) sts, leaving a 6-inch length of yarn to sew seam.

THUMB:

On 1st needle, K4 from holder; on 2nd needle, K2 (3-3) from holder and pick up 2 from cast on edge; on 3rd needle pick up 4 (5-5) from cast on edge. Work 14 (16-20) rounds even on these 12 (14-14) st.

Next row: *K2tog, repeat around. Break off yarn, leaving 6 inches. Draw yarn through remaining sts twice and fasten securely.

FINISHING:

Sew fingertip seam.

Trevor's Sweater

This is a basic set-in sleeve pattern that you can adapt in a number of ways to use small amounts of pet yarn.

You can knit up a sweater with store-bought wool—and use petspun to make stripes, a Fair Isle design, or even a picture of your dog. Kendall's mother knit this version for Kendall's son Trevor using two-ply Great Pyrenees as the main color and two-ply Newfoundland for the dog design. The yarn is quite bulky, and the sweater is nice and warm for sledding and walks in the snow.

We've included patterns for a few of our favorite dogs, and one for a cat, if that's what your petspun yarn dictates. We encourage you to design your own pet, using regular graph paper or graph paper designed specifically for knitters, available at most craft stores.

Trevor loves the dog sweater made by his grandmother, Patricia Crolius.

Sizes

Child's 6 (8-10)
Finished chest measurement 29 (31-33) inches

Materials

Yarn: 15 (18-19) ounces bulky weight yarn; approximately 315 yards of main color for size 6, 15 yards of contrasting color for dog pictured

Straight needles, sizes 9 and 10

Gauge: 4 stitches per inch in stockinette stitch, with larger needles

Instructions

BACK:

With smaller needles, cast on 55 (59-63) sts. Work in K1, P1 ribbing for 1½ (2-2) inches, inc 3 sts evenly across the last row to give 58 (62-66) sts. Change to larger needles and work in st st for rest of back. At 9½ (10½-11¼) inches begin armhole shaping: bind off 4 sts at beg of next 2 rows, then dec 1 st each edge every other row 3 (3-4) times to leave 44 (48-50) sts. Work even until 6 (6½-6¾) inches above armhole.

Next row: bind off 13 (14-15) sts, work across next 18 (20-20) sts and leave on holder for back of neck, bind off rem sts.

FRONT:

With smaller needles, cast on 55 (59-63) sts. Work in K1, P1 ribbing for 1½ (2-2) inches, inc 3 sts evenly across the last row to give 58 (62-66) sts. Work even in st st for 2 inches, or desired length to beg of dog pattern, ending with a purl row.

Dog Pattern: Each dog pattern notes the width and height in stitches/rows. The stitch representing the "visual center" is marked on the pattern—this is not always the numerical center. With the right side of the work facing, begin the pattern, reading from right to left. Counting from the center stitch of the sweater body will indicate which stitch should start the dog pattern. If you create your own animal pattern, be sure that the width in stitches is several inches less than the total width of the sweater. For the height, be sure that you take into account where the armhole decreases will occur, in order to leave room for the whole dog!

Continue to work as for back until work measures 4½ (4½-4¾) inches above armhole.

Shape Neck: With right side facing, work 16 (18-19) sts and leave remaining sts on holder. To work shaping, dec 1 st at neck edge every other row 3 (4-4) times. Work even on rem 13 (14-15) sts until front is same length

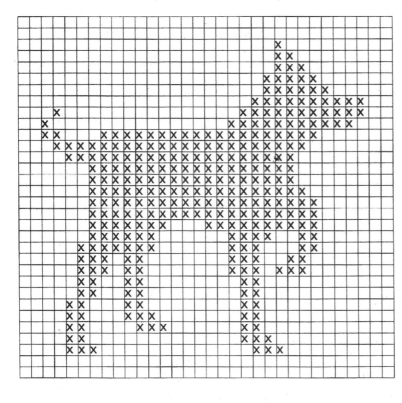

Read diagrams from right to left, and repeat the pattern around the row. When working with two colors of yarn, carry the second yarn loosely in back, and twist the yarn in use around the yarn you carry every three stitches.

Start here

as back to shoulder, and bind off. To complete other side, leave center 12 sts on holder for front of neck and work on rem sts as for first side.

SLEEVES:

With smaller needles, cast on 25 (27-29) sts. Work in K1, P1 ribbing for 2 inches, inc 11 (13-13) sts evenly across last row to give 36 (40-42) sts. Change to larger needles and work in st st for remainder of sleeve. Inc 1 st each edge every 2¼ (2⅓-2⅔) inches, 4 (4-5) times, to give a total of 44 (48-52) sts. Work even until 11½ (13-14½) inches from beg, or desired length to underarm.

Shape Cap: Bind off 4 sts at beg of next 2 rows, then dec 1 st at each end of every other row until 12 (14-14) sts remain. Then bind off 2 sts at beg of next 4 rows. Bind off remaining 4 (6-6) sts.

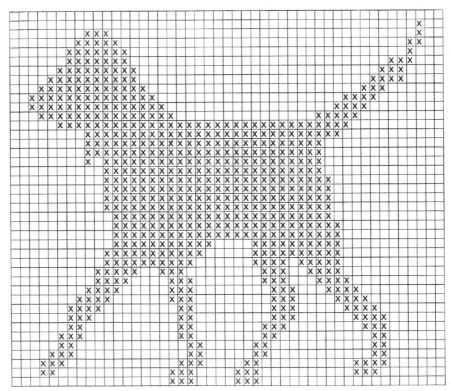

Start here

NECKBAND:

Sew right shoulder seam. With smaller needles, pick up and K 8 (10-10) sts on side of neck, work across 12 sts from front holder, pick up and K 9 (11-11) sts on other side on neck, work across 18 (20-20) sts from back holder, for a total of 47 (53-53) sts. Work in K1, P1 ribbing for 1 inch. Bind off all sts loosely.

FINISHING:

Sew left shoulder seam and neckband. Set in sleeves at armhole openings. Sew underarm and side seams.

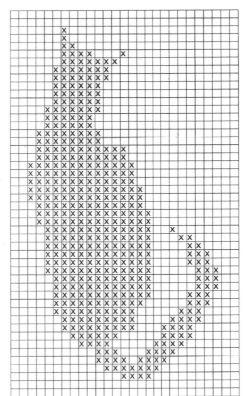

Start here ←

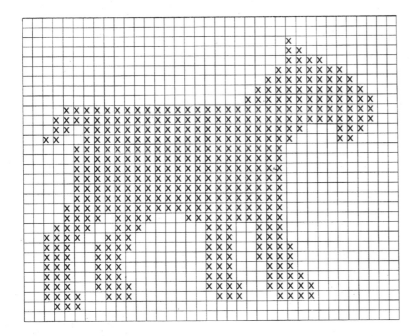

Start here ←

Peg Fyffe's Blue-Ribbon Pullover

This gorgeous sweater, created by Peg Fyffe, took first place at the 1992 Indiana State Fair in the handspun category. Peg spun the hair from three cats—Persian and Standard Breeds—and dyed a few skeins spruce-green so she'd have three colors to work with. Peg used a commercial pattern, and we have developed a similar pattern you can use to make a similar sweater.

Peg Fyffe proudly displays the cat yarn sweater that took the blue ribbon at the Indiana State Fair.

Sizes

Men's 42 (44-46)

Materials

Yarn: Bulky yarn, 20 (22-24) ounces main color (A); 8 (10-12) ounces EACH of colors B and C

Straight needles, sizes 5 and 8 (or sizes required for gauge)

Stitch holders

Gauge: 4 stitches per inch in stockinette stitch, with larger needles

Instructions

PATTERN:

Work over 16 rows. When slipping stitches on knit rows, hold yarn in back. When slipping stitches on purl rows, hold yarn in front.
Row 1: Color B. Knit across.
Row 2: Color B. Purl across.
Row 3: Color A. K1, *slip 2, K2, repeat from *, ending slip 2, K1.
Row 4: Color A. P1, *slip 2, P2, repeat from *, ending slip 2, P1.

Row 5: Color A. Knit across.
Row 6: Color A. Purl across.
Row 7: Color C. K3, *slip 2, K2, repeat from *, ending slip 2, K3.
Row 8: Color C. Purl across.
Row 9: Color C. Knit across.
Row 10: Color C. Purl across.
Row 11: Color A. K1, *slip 2, K2, repeat from *, ending slip 2, K1.
Row 12: Color A. P1, *slip 2, P2, repeat from *, ending slip 2, P1.
Row 13: Color A. Knit across.
Row 14: Color A. Purl across.
Row 15: Color B. K3, *slip 2, K2, repeat from *, ending slip 2, K3.
Row 16: Color B. Purl across.

BACK:

With smaller needles and Color A, cast on 78 (82-86) sts. Work in K1, P1 ribbing for 2¼ inches. On last row, inc 10 sts evenly spaced [86 (90-94)

sts on needle]. Change to larger needles and work in pattern until work measures 18 (18¼-18½) inches, or desired length to underarm.

Armholes: (Note: Work in established pattern stitch while shaping).
Row 1: Bind off 3 sts at each edge.
Row 2: Bind off 2 sts at each edge.
Row 3: Bind off 1 st at each edge [76 (80-84) sts remaining].

Work even until work measures 10 (10¼-10½) inches above first armhole decrease.

Shoulders: Bind off 25 (27-29) sts at armhole edge. Put remaining sts on holder.

FRONT:

Work as for back until work measures 18 (18¼-18½) inches, ending with a purl row. On last row, place a marker in the center of the row.

Armhole and Neck Shaping:
Row 1: BO3, work to 2 sts before center marker, K2tog. Join second ball of yarn, sl1, K1, PSSO, K to last 3 st, BO3. Continue on both halves simultaneously.
Row 2: BO2, work to center. Left half, work to last 3 sts, BO2.
Row 3: BO1, work to center. Right half, work to last 2 sts, BO1.
Row 4: Dec 1 st at each neck edge. Repeat neck dec every 3rd row 11 more times [25 (27-29) sts remaining]. Work even until front equals length of back to shoulders. BO25 (27-29).

SLEEVES:

With Color A and smaller needles, cast on 27 (31-31) sts. Work in K1, P1 ribbing for 2 inches. On last row, inc 17 sts evenly spaced [44 (48-48) sts on needle]. Change to larger needles and begin pattern, increasing 1 st at each edge every 4 rows 17 times [78 (82-82) sts on needle]. Work even until sleeve measures 21¾ (22¼-22¾) inches or desired length to shoulder. Bind off all sts.

FINISHING:

Sew seam at right shoulder. With Color A and smaller needles, start at left side of neck and pick up evenly and K around neck, marking st at center of "V" and ending with sl st from holder for back of neck. Working in K1, P1 ribbing, dec 1 st on either side of the st at center of "V" until ribbing measures 1¼ inches. Bind off in ribbing.

Sew sleeves into armholes and sew side seams and sleeve seams as one.

Detta's Cardigan Sweater

Detta Juusola of Detta's Spindle in Maple Plain, Minnesota, created this beautiful sweater. The yarn is two-ply, with a strand of Samoyed plied with a strand of Corriedale wool. Detta is one of those accomplished knitters who no longer uses a pattern, but she referred us to *The Knitter's Design Sourcebook* by Hélène Rush, which we highly recommend. This pattern is from the book, and we are grateful to Down East Books in Camden, Maine, for granting permission to include it here.

Detta Juusola's beautiful cardigan sweater of Samoyed, modeled by Kendall's sister, Cynthia.

Materials

Yarn: 18 (20-22-24-26) ounces worsted weight

Straight needles, sizes 5 and 7 (or sizes required for gauge)

5 stitch holders

6 buttons

Gauge: 5 stitches per inch in stockinette stitch, with larger needles

Instructions

(These directions are for a woman's cardigan. For a man's sweater, work the buttonholes on the left front band rather than the right.)

Sizes	To Fit	Finished Measurement
Ladies' Small	32"	37"
Ladies' Medium	34"	39"
Ladies' Large/Men's Small	36"	41"
Men's Medium	38"	43"
Men's Large	40"	45"

BACK:

With smaller needles, cast on 85 (89-95-99-105) sts. Row 1: K1, *P1, K1. Row 2: P1, *K1, P1. Continue working in rib for 2½ inches, inc 6 sts evenly across last row to give 91 (95-101-105-111) sts. Use larger needles and work in st st for rest of back. At 15 (15½-16-16½-17) inches from beg, shape armhole: Bind off 5 sts at beg of next 2 rows, then dec 1 st at each end of every other row 5 times to leave 71 (75-81-85-91) sts.

Work even until 7 (7½-8-8½-9) inches above armhole. Next row, work across 22 (23-25-26-28) sts and leave on holder, work across next 27 (29-31-33-35) sts and leave on holder for back of neck, work on remaining sts and leave on holder.

LEFT FRONT:

With smaller needles, cast on 49 (51-53-55-59) sts. Row 1: *K1, P1; rep from * to last 5 sts, K5 for garter stitch band. Row 2: K5, *K1, P1; rep from * to end of row. Work these 2 rows for 2½ inches, inc 2 (2-3-3-2) sts evenly across last row (taking care not to work increases in garter st band) to give 51 (53-56-58-61) sts.

Using larger needles, work in st st for rest of front, continuing the garter st band on 5 sts as established. At 15 (15½-16-16½-17) inches from beg, shape armhole as for back, ending up with 41 (43-46-48-51) sts. At 4½ (5-5½-6-6½) inches above armhole, shape neck: With right side facing, work on 27 (28-30-31-33) sts and leave remaining 14 (15-16-17-18) sts on holder. To work shaping, dec 1 st

at neck edge every other row 5 times. Work even on remaining 22 (23-25-26-28) sts until front is same length as back to shoulder. Leave sts on holder.

RIGHT FRONT:

Cast on as for left side. Row 1: K5, *P1, K1; rep from * to end of row. Row 2: *P1, K1; rep from * to last 5 sts, K5 for garter stitch band. Work these 2 rows once more. With right side facing, K1, K2tog, YO, K2, work to end of row as established—first buttonhole made. Complete right side to match left side, evenly spacing 5 more buttonholes in garter st band and planning to work a 7th one in center of 1-inch neckband.

SLEEVES:

With smaller needles, cast on 41 (43-43-45-45) sts. Work in K1, P1 ribbing as for lower back for 2½ inches, inc 14 (14-16-16-18) sts evenly across last row to give 55 (57-59-61-63) sts. Use larger needles and work in st st for rest of sleeve. Inc 1 st at each end every 1⅔ (1¾-1¾-1¾-1¾) inches 8 (8-8-8-9) times to give a total of 71 (73-75-77-81) sts. Work even until 16½ (17-17½-18-18½) inches from beg, or desired length to underarm.

SHAPE CAP:

Bind off 5 sts at beg of next 2 rows, then dec 1 st at each end of every other row until 43 (43-43-39-39) sts remain. Then dec 2 sts at each end of every other row until 19 sts remain.

Bind off 3 sts at beg of next 4 rows. Bind off remaining 7 sts.

NECKBAND:

Knit shoulder seams sts together. With smaller needles, work across 14 (15-16-17-18) sts from right front holder, pick up and K 15 sts on right side of neck, work across 27 (29-31-33-35) sts from back holder, pick up and K 15 sts on other side of neck, work across 14 (15-16-17-18) sts from left front holder, for a total of 85 (89-93-97-101) sts. Keeping first and last 5 sts in garter st, work in K1, P1 rib on center sts. At one-half inch from beg, work last buttonhole, then work until band is 1 inch wide. Bind off all sts.

FINISHING:

Set in sleeves at armhole openings. Sew underarm and side seams. Sew buttons opposite buttonholes.

Jerie Lucas's Knitted and Woven Jacket

This beautiful jacket was designed and created by Jerie Lucas, who is probably the foremost expert on dog fibers in the country! Jerie is a master spinner, and earned her Certificate of Excellence from the Handweaver's Guild of America for her study titled "The Versatility of Dog Hair." The jacket is made from the hair of a Samoyed–Golden Retriever cross.

This garment is not only exquisite, it also demonstrates the versatility of the fibers, as it incorporates both knitting and weaving. We are most grateful to Jerie for allowing us to include it, and for all of her help and advice as we put together this book.

Size

Ladies' Medium

Materials

For woven fabric: 16/2 commercial yarn for warp, 80% wool/20% angora

dog hair yarn (singles) for weft*

4 harness Jack-type loom

sett: 12 epi

shots: 16 ppi

For knitted sleeves and collar: 2-ply dog yarn, worsted weight*

Studio Bulky knitting machine

Gauge: 4 stitches per inch, 5½ rows per inch.

*A total of 16 ounces of dog yarn was used for this jacket.

Jerie Lucas's knitted and woven jacket from Yosha, a Samoyed–Golden Retriever cross. (Photo courtesy of Shuttle, Spindle and Dyepot, *The Handweavers Guild of America, Lisa Clayton, photographer.)*

A commercial sewing pattern for a jacket can help you shape neck opening and armholes, if desired.

Instructions

WEAVING:

The loom was threaded twill and treadled tabby. A wide sett was used so the fabric is almost weft-faced. Width of fabric should be approximately 24 inches, and the length of finished fabric should be approximately 54 inches, or twice the desired length of jacket.

After removing the fabric from the loom, wash by hand and spin gently in washing machine. Lay flat to dry.

Fold fabric in half, with fold at

shoulders (there is no sewn seam necessary at shoulders). Mark center front to the fold. Mark neck opening and armholes. Mark fabric to taper slightly from the jacket bottom to the underarms. Before cutting, machine stitch on either side of lines, using a short straight stitch. Cut fabric on lines. Cut pockets from fabric removed for armholes.

KNITTING:

Follow diagrams for machine knitting the sleeves and collar. For seam bind-ing, cast on 5 sts and knit the required length to cover the raw edges of the woven fabric at side seams and around pockets.

The knitted collar and sleeves are machine stitched to the outside of the woven pieces, and hand-sewn to the inside.

The elasticity of the knitting allows the collar to form a soft roll, and helps prevent the elbows from bagging. The smoother finish of the woven fabric using a wool warp adds contrast and a tailored look.

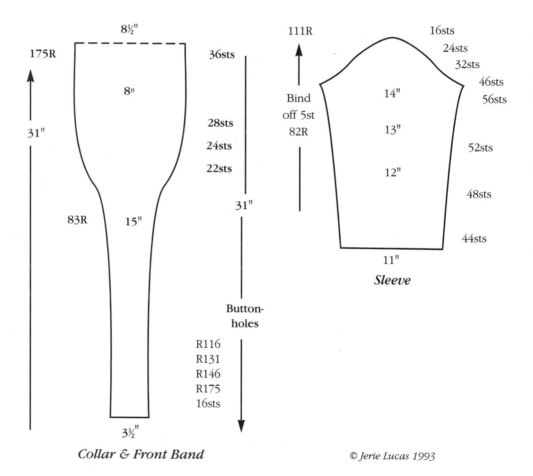

Collar & Front Band

Sleeve

© *Jerie Lucas 1993*

Dog Sweater

Every sweater in this book could accurately be described as a dog sweater, but this time we mean a sweater for a dog to wear. While this may strike you as a bit redundant, think how thrilled your Pekingese would be to dress up like a Saint Bernard.

This sweater was designed for Barkley, a Pug belonging to Kendall's neighbors, Cindy and Dan Forbes. It's knit of two-ply Newfoundland yarn, and Cindy and Dan swear the sweater elevates Barkley's self-esteem.

Barkley let his mate, Gizmo, model his Newfoundland costume. Gizmo thinks it's her mink.

SIZES

Small, to fit a Yorkie: Neck 8½ inches, Chest 11 inches

Medium, to fit a Toy Poodle: Neck 10 inches, Chest 15 inches

Large, to fit a Pug: Neck 17 inches, Chest 22 inches

Instructions are for size Small (Medium and Large in parentheses).

Materials

Yarn: 1½ (2¼-5¼) ounces yarn

Straight needles, sizes 5 and 6 (or sizes required for gauge)

Double-pointed and circular needles in smaller size

Gauge: 4 stitches per inch in stockinette stitch, with larger needles

Instructions

Starting at neck edge, with smaller needles cast on 34 (42-70) sts. Work in K2, P2 ribbing for 1½ (1½-2) inches.

Change to larger needles. Work 2 rows in st st. Then inc 1 st at each edge every row 4 (4-7) times, then 1 st at each edge every other row 4 (4-8) times [50 (58-98) sts on needle].

LEG HOLES:

With right side facing, K5 (6-9), BO5 (6-8), K30 (34-64), BO5 (6-8), K5 (6-9).

Next row: P5 (6-9). Continue in st st on these 5 (6-9) sts only for 4 (6-8) more rows. Break off yarn and place these 5 (6-9) sts on holder.

Join yarn to center section and P30

(34-64). Continue working st st on this section for 4 (6-8) more rows. Break off yarn and place these stitches on a holder.

Join yarn to last section and P5 (6-9). Continue in st st for 4 (6-8) more rows.

Joining row: K5 (6-9), CO5 (6-8), K30 (34-64) sts from holder, CO5 (6-8), K5 (6-9) sts from holder [50 (58-98) sts on needle]. Work even in st st until work measures 5 (5½-9) inches, or desired length to end of rib cage, ending with a purl row.

Bind off 6 (7-12) sts at beg of next 2 rows [38 (44-74) sts rem]. Dec 1 st at each edge every other row 7 (7-11) times [24 (30-52) sts rem].

Work even in st st until work measures 10 (11-13½) inches or 1 (1¼-1¼) inches less than desired length to base of tail, ending with a purl row. Place all sts on a holder.

FINISHING:

Sew seam from neck edge to bind off rows. With circular needle, K 24 (30-52) sts from holder, then pick up evenly and knit around back opening, for a total number of stitches that is a multiple of 4. Work K2, P2 ribbing for 1 (1¼-1¼) inches and bind off in ribbing.

With double-pointed needles, pick up and K 16 (16-28) sts at leg hole. Work in K2, P2 ribbing for 1 inch. Bind off in ribbing. Repeat for other leg hole.

Sew elastic on sweater in front of dog's rear legs if desired.

9

Care of Your Finished Garment

You've done it! You are now the proud creator and owner of a truly unique petspun garment. You'll be admired by your friends, and your dog or cat will be the envy of all the pets in the neighborhood.

How do you take care of your masterpiece? You can wash your pet-spun products the same way you would wash any fine washable woolen: hand-wash in lukewarm water with a mild soap or detergent. You don't need to use dog shampoo for your finished garment—once you have the pet smell out of the fibers, it won't come back—unless, of course, your pet borrows the garment for a special soirée.

Because petspun yarn is less elastic than wool, knitted or crocheted items have a tendency to lose their shape when they get wet. There are several things you can do to minimize distortion. After rinsing the garment, let the water drain completely from the sink. Leaving your item in the sink, gently squeeze it to remove as much water as possible. Then lift it carefully, supporting it so that the full weight of the damp yarn does not pull the garment out of shape. Place your creation on a clean towel and roll it up, pressing gently to extract as much moisture as possible.

Lay your work on a dry towel and gently straighten it into its proper shape. Let it dry flat, away from direct heat and sunlight.

We don't recommend machine washing, even on a gentle cycle,

because garments can be pulled out of shape by the vigorous churning action of the machine.

Dry cleaning is certainly an option, if you dare to trust your handiwork to the hands of another. We can never bring ourselves to do that.

With proper care, your petspun garment will last for years. It will be a treasured heirloom for generations.

10

The Spinner's Guide to Dog Breeds

It is not too difficult to evaluate your pet on the basis of his or her yarn potential. Simply pick some fuzz off your clothes and check it out. The key criteria are softness and length of fiber.

We divide the dog world into three broad categories. In descending order of desirability they are: those whose coats can be spun solo; those whose coats should be blended with longer fibers; and those whose short coats can be "sprinkled" on longer fibers.

Solo: The crème de la crème! As a rule, fibers two inches in length and longer are spinnable on their own. The very softest yarn comes from long undercoat fibers, but several breeds' topcoats are soft enough to

make a nice yarn. If you prefer a yarn that is more elastic, you can blend or ply these breeds with wool; we enjoy the satisfaction of going completely to the dogs, working with pure, unadulterated pooch.

Blend: These are fibers between one and two inches long. While an experienced spinner can spin them solo, they are not recommended for novice spinners. They tend to yield yarn that breaks rather easily, particularly if there is not enough twist given to the yarn. Many of these fibers are extremely soft, however, and make a delightful fuzzy yarn when blended with wool during carding.

Sprinkle: Our position is that there is no such thing as an utterly unspinnable dog. (The Mexican Hairless is, perhaps, the exception that proves the rule.) In deference to the owners of short-haired breeds—you know who you are: the ones who always smugly tell the rest of us that your dog doesn't shed at all—we have included a technique for incorporating your beloved's fibers into yarn. We call it "sprinkling," and it involves painstakingly collecting the little hairs from your pet and sprinkling them onto wool or another longer fiber of a contrasting color. This doesn't make the most spectacular yarn in the world. We freely admit that this procedure is *only* for the obsessive owner who is determined to sport a garment to which Rover contributed. We know such people, and *they* feel this is worth it.

Still not sure which category your canine falls into? No problem—the following list includes every breed we've ever heard of. (Some breeds are popularly known by more than one name, such as the Borzoi, also known as a Russian Wolfhound. We have tried to include alternate designations for breeds where appropriate.) Most of the breeds listed are recognized by at least one of the major Western kennel clubs—the American Kennel Club, the Canadian Kennel Club, the Australian National Kennel Council, the Kennel Club (Great Britain), the Kennel Union of South Africa, or the European Fédération Cynologique Internationale (the F.C.I., which represents two Asian, one African, nineteen European, and twelve Latin American countries). If your baby is not included, write to us pronto and we'll stick him or her into the revised edition.

We've spun fuzz from all the breeds we could get our hands on and consulted with groomers on the coat characteristics of the rest. You should note that fuzz can vary within the same breed, and even from dog to dog in the same litter. Generally, female fuzz will be a bit softer than male, light fuzz often softer than dark, and puppy fuzz the softest of all. Ironically, coats that aren't regularly groomed will offer better spinning material than those of dogs who are regularly stripped.

The breed listings that follow reflect the "ideal" coat for each breed but may not perfectly describe the consistency of the fuzz you collect from your pet. As always, your fingers are your best guide.

Affenpinscher

Also known as the "monkey dog," this lively little guy has an abundant, wiry coat, best suited for adding strength and durability to a softer yarn.

Afghan Hound

It would be a cinch to make an afghan from your Afghan. These elegant creatures feature thick, long, and silky coats in a plethora of luscious colors such as apricot, cream-red, and platinum. A spinner's delight.

Airedale

These versatile creatures have terrific personalities, but they produce less than ideal spinning material. They are protected by a stiff, dense outercoat—which may be crinkly or a bit wavy—and a softer, dense undercoat. The undercoat is short, and should be blended with another longer fiber to spin.

Akita (a.k.a. Shishi Inu)

Sort out the stiff outercoat of this Japanese hunter and go for the fine, thick undercoat, which is generally too short to spin solo but spins nicely blended with longer fibers.

Alaskan Malamute

If you ever wondered what keeps these babies warm during sled expeditions to the Arctic (besides, of course, ferocious quantities of aerobic exercise) simply grab a comb and strip out some of their thick, downy undercoat. This stuff will keep you toasty.

American Water Spaniel

The closely curled or "marcel-effect" coat protects this puppy in the water, and it can be blended with longer fibers to protect you in inclement weather.

Anatolian Shepherd

This rare, flock-guarding, mastiff-like breed hails from Turkey and is enormous—males stand some thirty-two inches at the shoulders. Their coats range from short and coarse (sprinkle only) to long and soft. Our sample was of the latter variety, which can be blended or spun solo.

Anglo-Français

The most popular pack hound in France has a shiny, short coat totally unsuited for spinning. Do not despair. Sprinkle it on wool or any longer fiber and—*voilà!*—Jacques can be worn to your favorite café, *à la mode.*

Australian Cattle Dog (a.k.a. Blue or Australian Heeler)

A short, cottony, dense undercoat beneath a tough outercoat is blendable with longer fibers. These are intelligent, hard-working dogs, capable of inspiring great devotion in their owners.

Australian Kelpie (a.k.a. Barb)

The Kelpie, an Australian Collie, and the most common working sheepdog in Australia and New Zealand, isn't one for much fuss. You may get him to sit still through a grooming if the sheep are behaving themselves. He has a short double coat, and his dense undercoat should be blended with longer fibers for best results.

Australian Terrier

This rabbit- and rat-hunting dog has a shaggy, straight coat, a stiff, dense outer coat, and a slight, soft undercoat that is best blended.

Basenji (a.k.a. Congo Terrier, Barkless Dog)

We're sorry. This dog has always confused us. It yodels instead of barks, trots like a horse, and licks itself clean like a cat. And its short, silky hair is best suited for blending with other fibers. It is redeemed, however, by its cheerful temperament.

Basset Hound

Dear, dear. Sprinkle the short, smooth hairs on a longer, more spinnable fiber and content yourself with the fact that you have an incredibly lovable dog. It's something about that lugubrious expression.

Beagle

Although Beagles possess a short, dense coat best suited for sprinkling, these dogs are great pets, and the plethora of Snoopy patterns makes this breed irresistible.

Beauceron (a.k.a. Berger de Beauce)

This protective sheepherder of French origin is found primarily in Continental Europe, where it is also used as a hunting and guard dog. It has a very short, downy, thick undercoat that should be blended with other fibers.

Bedlington Terrier (a.k.a. Gypsy Dog)

With its wonderful resemblance to a lamb, it is no surprise that this creature has a wooly undercoat. Since Bedlingtons are closely clipped during grooming, it's best to harvest when they have been left au naturel for a while. Colors are blue, blue and tan, sandy, or liver.

Belgian Shepherd Dogs

The long-haired varieties are the Groenendael and the Tervuren, which both boast long, smooth hair about the body and thick ruffs about the neck and chest, all of which is easy to harvest and makes a very soft yarn. The short-haired Malinois has a dense undercoat that is best blended, and the Laekenois offers a thick, woolly undercoat, easy to spin once the harsh outercoat has been picked out.

Berger Picard (a.k.a. Picardy Sheepdog)

A harsh, brittle outercoat protects a lovely, soft, blendable undercoat of fine, dense hair in this hardworking breed. All shades of gray and tawny colors.

Bernese Mountain Dogs

Prized by the Romans as fighting dogs, and used by the Swiss as tireless cattle dogs, these gorgeous creatures have an abundance of long, silky, slightly wavy hair to spin into something wonderful. The jet-black coats, highlighted by white and red markings, are exceptionally glossy.

Bichon Frise (a.k.a. Teneriffe)

Great spinning material on this fluffy little guy—he boasts both white, silky, loosely curled hair in his outercoat and a soft, cottony undercoat.

Black-and-Tan Coonhound

Ah, the melodious bay of the Coonhound! Unfortunately, his voice is neater than his short, dense coat, at least from a spinner's point of view. Sprinkle only.

Black Russian Terrier (a.k.a. Chornyi)

Only our wonderful groomer, Elizabeth Emanuel, could have provided fuzz from these incredibly rare dogs (there are no more than fifty or so of them in the entire United States). Built like Barkley from "Sesame Street," with a light-footed, rolling, high-energy gait, these big guys have wonderful spinning coats: thick, three to four-inch-long outercoats supplemented by a lush undercoat (maybe they're why spinning dog hair is so popular in Russia). Spinners unite! We need more of these Soviet sweeties in the States!

Bleu de Gascogne (Grand and Basset)

Sacre Bleu! What superb noses, eh? *Hélas,* the coats of these French hounds may only be sprinkled amid longer fibers—something that won't offend their keen olfactory senses.

Bloodhound

Also known by its Belgian name, the Saint Hubert, this dignified creature is a bust as a fuzz provider. Sprinkle the short, dense hairs among longer fibers to honor your pet, who undoubtedly richly deserves it.

Border Terrier
Recognized by the British Kennel Club in 1920, this scrappy fellow has a rough coat that is not ideal for spinning, but the thick undercoat can be blended with longer fibers.

Borzoi (a.k.a. Russian Wolfhound)
These imposing beasts have feathering on their forelegs and chest, as well as abundant, slightly coarse, curlier neck hair suitable for blending. Borzoi come in many colors.

Boston Terrier (a.k.a. Round Head)
No more suited for spinning than Boston baked beans, these brindled pets are sprinkle candidates only. We think something tea-colored would be most appropriate.

Bouvier des Flandres
Anne says these are the Very Best Dogs in the World, and one, Irish, was instru-

Anne with her brace of Bouvier puppies, Quiche's Teddy Roosevelt and Quiche's Lucy Raffles. These Very Best Puppies will grow up to be Very Best Dogs. (Janis Jaquith, photographer.)

mental in bringing our two coauthors together (Irish used to play with Kendall's Golden Retriever, Abby, and friendships were struck all around). And although they may look like unmade beds, Bouviers are possessed of an admirably thick, soft undercoat that just begs to be spun into something warm and, like the dog, practical. A sturdy scarf, perhaps. Or given the impressive quantity of fluff, a lap robe. Colors range from black to fawn, with many brindled or gray.

Boxer
Although Boxers are devoted and loving guard dogs, their coats are not good for much except sprinkling. The short, hard hair lies close to the dog's body.

Bracco Italiano
A breed that can be traced to the Middle Ages, this Italian pointer is virtually unknown in the United States. Unfortunately, its short, shiny coat will not make it a favorite among spinners. If you own a Bracco, we suggest the sprinkle technique.

Braque d'Auvergne, Braque Français, Braque Saint-Germain
These are all types of French pointers. All are excellent bird dogs but possess lousy coats for spinning. Sprinkle only.

Briard
Now this is a coat worth harvesting. The outercoat is about three inches long, and the texture is dry and a bit coarse. The undercoat is delightfully soft. Owners tend to be devoted to these happy, hard-working creatures, and will undoubtedly think of a suitable application for their fuzz.

Brittany Spaniel
The fine, thick, slightly wavy hair on these gifted hunting dogs should be

blended with longer fibers for the best results.

Bulldog
Yes, they look like Churchill. No, there's not much to spin. Sprinkle while humming "God Save the Queen"—these are noble beasts.

Bulldog (French)
The French Bulldog is a good deal smaller than its British cousin, and its coat offers a similarly poor harvest. Sprinkle to "La Marseillaise" for good measure.

Bullmastiff
Lousy coat for spinning, but we're not about to tell him. These guys weigh in at about 130 pounds, virtually none of it hair. Sprinkle respectfully.

Bull Terrier
This muscular little guy offers little to an eager harvester. Some dogs may present a soft undercoat in winter that would be suitable for spinning with longer fibers. Otherwise, sprinkle.

Cairn Terrier
Your basic double coat—a thick, harsh outercoat and a softer (though still slightly coarse) blendable undercoat. If the critter were bigger, harvesting would be a tad easier. But nothing about this cocky dog is easy, so its owners are probably used to a bit of trouble. Lovely colors ranging from cream through red, gray, and nearly black.

Cavalier King Charles Spaniel
You can get some decent, though not copious, fuzz from this cheerful pet. The CKCS has soft, silky, straight fur, and it comes in some interesting color combinations for heather yarns.

Chesapeake Bay Retriever
Since the Chesapeake spends significant amounts of time in the water, it's not surprising to discover that his coat is oilier than that of most other breeds. His outercoat is about an inch and a half long, harsh and oily, and the undercoat is dense and woolly. Both are blendable.

Chihuahua
Well, it's going to take you a long, long time to get much out of these guys. The smooth-coated ones will produce sprinkle material. And with enormous perseverance, you will probably harvest enough from the long-haired variety to make, say, a nosewarmer.

Chinese Crested Dog
Like the Mexican Hairless, this dog has no fur at all, with the exception of a flowing crest of silky hair on top of its head. If you think Mr. Chihuahua was a challenge, just try harvesting sufficient spinning material from this guy.

Chinook
This rare American sled dog is a lovely tawny color; its thick, blendable undercoat is one to one and a half inches long, and blows, as one would expect, before the summer heat hits.

Chow Chow
These bearlike beasts have been bred in China for some two thousand years, and the coat is a spinner's delight. First of all, it's abundant. Really abundant. The rough-coated variety boasts a dense, straight coat with a harsh outercoat and a soft, woolly undercoat. The coat of the smooth-coated Chow is plentiful, dense, and plush. Solid colors include white, cream, tawny red, blue, and black. These guys blow coat with a vengeance in the spring.

Clumber Spaniel
Although these British dogs are not well known in the United States, they're so

good-natured and lovable they probably should be. They have a good coat for spinning, featuring lots of silky, straight hair.

Cocker Spaniel (American)
Who could forget the elegant Lady, of *Lady and the Tramp* fame? The long, silky fur is wonderful to work with, makes supersoft yarn, and there's plenty of it, especially during shedding season. Many glossy colors available.

Cocker Spaniel (English)
Another silky, glossy-coated dog, the English Cocker is slightly larger than its American counterpart. Same wonderful range of colors, dense hair.

Collie
Great stuff, here. Rough Collies have a dense, stiff outercoat and a lovely thick undercoat—it's the soft, fluffy stuff you want to spin. Smooth Collie undercoat is short and may be best combined with longer fibers. Both Bearded and Border Collies also offer thick, soft undercoats— the former is eminently spinnable; the latter, blendable.

Curly-Coated Retriever
This wetlands warrior's tightly curled, black or liver-colored coat might be blended with another fiber or perhaps merely sprinkled in with longer stuff.

Dachsbracke
This popular Swedish breed, recognized by the Canadian Kennel Club, has a very slight undercoat. Sprinkle with love.

Dachshund (a.k.a. Teckel)
The long-haired version of this short-legged beastie offers decent blending material from its soft, silky coat. The wirehaired breeds have short, rough coats intermingled with some finer hairs, but picking the latter out would try the patience of Job and probably bring your sanity into question. Like the Short-Haired Dachshund owner, you are best off sprinkling some of your pet's hair amidst a longer, more spinnable fiber.

Dalmatian
Known as the "Coach Dog" in England and the "Fire Engine Dog" in the United States, this black-and-white spotted canine has a hard, shiny coat totally unsuitable for spinning. Sprinkle liberally among longer fibers.

Dandie Dinmont Terrier
Decent harvest for a terrier, especially from the underbelly, where the fuzz is softer and lighter. The coat should be fuzzy, as will be most anything spun from it. Pick out those guard hairs!

Deerhound (a.k.a. Scottish Deerhound)
Fuzz can be harvested from this shaggy beast, which was once known as "the royal dog of Scotland," but it isn't going to give the Afghan any competition. Blend.

Doberman Pinscher
Sweeter-tempered and far more loyal than its fearsome reputation would suggest, the Doberman is a terrible harvest prospect. Unless it's your dog, this is probably just as well. Sprinkle the short hairs liberally among wool and watch the urban predators back right off.

Dogue de Bordeaux
With a face only its mother could love (think of Hooch of the film *Turner and Hooch*), this rare French mastiff is no better a fuzz provider than its English counterpart. Sprinkle with longer fibers.

Elkhound (a.k.a. Norwegian Elkhound)
Now we're getting some serious fuzz. The most popular dog in Norway boasts a wonderfully thick, soft, woolly, gray undercoat. The poor beast can't stand the

heat, and will shed profusely in the late spring, to the delight of spinners everywhere. (Some find the fuzz a bit short and easier to spin when blended with longer fibers.)

English Pointer
This exemplary hunter has no spinnable coat at all. Sprinkle the short, hard hairs amid longer fibers and point to your dog's many other virtues.

English Setter (a.k.a. Laverack Setter)
Though lacking a wonderful undercoat, this willing hunter does provide a fairly soft topcoat to blend.

English Springer Spaniel
Cheerful and obedient, the Springer's coat offers a bit of hope—the water-repellent feathering on its legs and the longer hair on its ears and chest can be accumulated for blended spinning, although it helps if you're not in too great a hurry.

English Toy Spaniel (King Charles and Ruby, Blenheim and Prince Charles)
The King Charles boasts a glossy black-and-tan coat, while the Ruby is a chestnut red; both coats are fine spinning material—long, silky, and soft. The texture of the Blenheim and the Prince Charles spaniels is equally nice, but the shorter hair length may make these more suitable candidates for blending.

English Toy Terrier (a.k.a. Black-and-Tan Toy or Manchester Toy)
Dense, shiny, short hair must be sprinkled amid longer fibers to create something from this little guy.

Épagneul de Pont-Audemar
Like its relative, the Irish Water Spaniel, this breed offers a slightly pre-oiled coat that is thick and curly. Usually brown or brown and gray, this coat would blend

nicely to make a useful, all-weather beret.

Épagneul Français
This super gun dog has pretty decent blending material, with relatively long, fine, shiny hair, usually white marked with brown.

Épagneul Picard
Coarse and slightly curly hair make this coat suitable for outer-layer garments or to be mixed with something softer.

Eskimo Dog (Canadian Eskimo Dog, Grönlandshund)
Like the Alaskan Malamute, these guys have impossibly thick, soft undercoats, and they come in virtually all colors. Great blending material.

Eurasier
A new kid on the block, this breed combines Spitz and Chow Chow elements. Although its undercoat is wonderfully dense, it is a bit on the short side. It can be spun, but might be easier mixed with a longer fiber.

Field Spaniel
A marvelous sporting dog, this spaniel has a silky coat, although you will have to blend it to get decent spinning material.

Fila Brasileiro
These massive, mastifflike working dogs herd cattle and protect homes in their native Brazil—it's a rare thief who'll take on 100 to 175 pounds of dog. Scant blendable undercoat for the most devoted of human *amigos* to play with.

Finnish Spitz
The short, dense undercoat can be easily harvested from this breed, but you may want to mix it with longer fibers to facilitate spinning. This former bear hunter

comes in pretty shades of reddish gold and brown.

Flat-Coated Retriever
Flatties are a neat combo of Newf, Collie, and Setter blood, although their fine, medium-textured coats do not yield wonderful spinning stuff. It's best to mix this hair with a longer, more spinnable fiber that's compatible with its liver or black coloration.

Foxhound (American and English)
Ahem. Well, appropriate *patterns*, at least, will be plentiful—think of all those preppy hunting scenes. Sprinkle gently amid longer fibers and chuckle.

Fox Terrier
The Jimmy Cagney of the canine world, the Wirehaired Fox Terrier is a better fuzz prospect than its equally scrappy smooth-haired cousin. The WHFT's coat is springy and a bit coarse, spinnable for outerwear, and it also has a short, fluffy undercoat that can be blended with longer fibers.

François Blanc et Noir
Zut, alors! Sprinkle the chic black-and-white short hair with longer fibers or you will have *rien de tout* to spin.

Galgo
Neither the short, soft-coated variety nor the hard-coated variety of this Spanish greyhound produces spinning material. Sprinkle—and remember that the wily Spaniard Salvador Dali was a surrealist, too.

German Shepherd
You *vill* spin this dog's hair, and you *vill* enjoy it! Wonderfully multitalented, intelligent, and athletic, the German Shepherd is one of the most popular breeds in the world. These guys need a hard brushing to keep their thick double coats in fine form, but spinners will need to mix the short gray or fawn undercoat fuzz (collectible by the fistful in the spring) with longer fibers.

German Shorthaired Pointer (a.k.a. Kurzhaar)
A weekly grooming will yield little worth spinning from this lively, all-purpose hunting dog. Sprinkle the fallen hairs amid less difficult fibers and point with pride to the finished product—a camouflage scarf, perhaps.

German Wirehaired Pointer (a.k.a. Drahthaar)
A veritable canine stew of Pointer, Terrier, and Poodle, among others, the GWHP is a versatile hunter with harvesting possibilities. Its thick undercoat could be spun, but it's a tad short—easily mixed with lengthier stuff.

Golden Retriever
If an outrageously cheerful disposition and a deluxe undercoat were not enough to endear these dogs to spinners, the truly yummy shades of red and gold found in their coats would win one over. Kendall is especially fond of this breed, and was privileged to have shared her home with a gorgeous Golden, the late, great Abby.

The source of these mittens was a Golden Retriever named Thunder, so Karen Agee calls them "Thundermitts." (Photo courtesy of Karen Agee.)

Gordon Setter

This noble laddie of Scots ancestry offers a glossy, black, medium-length, blendable coat, silky in texture, with rich tan or mahogany markings. With a little effort (and some compatible wool), you could spin two yarns and weave a tartan.

Grand Spitz

Known as the Laika in Russia, the Grand Loulou in France, and the Volpino in Italy, the Grand Spitz is the official F.C.I. designation for the breed. It is distinguished from the Keeshond and the Wolf Spitz chiefly by color, and comes in black, white, or brown rather than the others' hallmark silvery gray. You will be awed by the fabulous, downy, thick undercoat that blows with a vengeance in the spring; plan to spin enough for a *big* project, like sweaters for the whole family.

Great Dane (a.k.a. German Mastiff)

Although males skyrocket to 32 inches at the shoulder, there is simply nothing from their short coats to spin. (You knew this, Horatio.) Sprinkle madly and recite soliloquies.

Great Pyrenees

Although the outercoat is slightly coarse, the thick, soft, white undercoat spins beautifully, and the best news is—there's plenty of it! These wonderful Pyrenean mountain dogs are big—reaching thirty-two inches—and sweet-tempered enough to let you harvest to your heart's content, especially in the spring, when they blow their coats.

Greyhound

Swift of foot, short of coat. Sprinkle the very short hairs amid longer fibers and hope they stay in.

Griffon (Belge, Bruxellois, and Petit Brabançon)

Rare outside their native Belgium, these former rat catchers have two coat textures: harsh and wiry in the Belge and Bruxellois Griffons (spinnable, but harsh on the skin); and short and sprinkable in the Petit Brabançon. The latter also has a light undercoat, but the fibers are awfully short.

Griffon Fauve de Bretagne

This rare French hound has a tough, wiry coat of fawn, with gold and reddish brown overtones. The likelihood of your owning one is *really* remote, but you could spin this stuff.

Griffon Nivernais

The wiry, dense, longer hair on this former boar hunter's coat can easily be spun but would be scratchy on the skin. Maybe that's why this beguiling beast has a sad expression. Its fuzz would certainly add strength to other fibers.

Griffon Vendéen (Grand)

The largest of the Vendéen Griffons, this fellow offers a dense undercoat, which can be stripped and spun, and an interesting long, wiry topcoat, usually two shades of tan, fawn, gray, or black, which could be spun to make a strong, coarse yarn.

Hanoverian Schweisshund

Rarely seen outside the land that gave us *bratwurst* and *wiener schnitzel*, this keen-scented hunter's thick, glossy coat is too short to spin. Sprinkle *mit* care *mit* longer fibers.

Harrier

This ancient coursing hound's smooth, flat, shortish hair needs a little help from his quarry—perhaps you could combine with a luxuriously long rabbit fur to create hare of the hound!

Ibizan Hound (a.k.a. Podenco Ibicenco or Charnique)

With a pedigree stretching back to the days of the Pharaohs, the Ibizan Hound is not short on impressive genealogy; it is, however, short on spinnable fuzz. Sprinkle the hairs with something equally rarefied, and make something to pass down through the ages.

Irish Setter (a.k.a. Red Setter)
Shiny, glossy, like dancing flame—this rich, red coat is too gorgeous *not* to spin! Harvest carefully from the silky feathers on the ears, legs, belly, and tail, and collect compendiums of compliments on your truly Irish sweater!

Irish Terrier
Another redhead, this gutsy beastie has a wiry topcoat and a slight, short, soft undercoat. The latter could be spun, but it will be necessary to mix the fuzz with longer fibers.

Irish Water Spaniel
Breeders recommend grooming this dog as little as possible, making harvesting difficult. The tightly curled, dark, liver-colored coat has a wonderfully bizarre purple tint to it, and it is naturally oily. Be patient, take a little fuzz at a time, and your pet will be none the worse for wear.

Irish Wolfhound
In days of yore, only kings, poets, and noblemen were permitted to own these splendid giants. Their rough, wiry hair, which comes in any number of colors, is not really suited for spinning, but their undercoats could be mixed with a longer fiber to fashion something impressive.

Italian Greyhound
Sprinkle the short, fine hair, which comes in shades of black, fawn, cream, red, or blue, with longer fibers. Since this creature is capable of reaching sixty kilometers per hour, work fast!

Italian Spinone (a.k.a. Italian Griffon, Italian Pointer)
It sounds like a dessert, but this is one great-looking dog. It has a rough, tousled coat, usually white with orange or reddish brown markings, that will yield a decent harvest—the yarn will be a bit coarse, and you may wish to combine it with longer, softer fibers.

Jack Russell Terrier
Although not an officially recognized breed by any of the kennel clubs, the Jack Russell's legions of fans couldn't give a flip—they know a doggy little dog when they see one. Spinners will have to blend these fibers with longer fibers—and don't count on a soft yarn!

Jagdterrier
This German terrier's harsh, tight, wiry coat does not provide much harvesting material. Brush, and sprinkle the yield with longer fibers.

Japanese Chin (a.k.a. Tchin or Japanese Spaniel)
Fabulous stuff—long, silky, straight hair and lots of it. These former playthings of the Japanese Imperial Court are tiny—a scant twelve inches tall—but their coats are so profuse that harvesting a sufficiency of fuzz shouldn't take too long. Chins are correctly colored red and white or black and white.

Keeshond (a.k.a. Dutch Barge Dog)
One of the best! These beauties don't just blow their coats, they positively explode in the spring! Huge handfuls of soft, downy fuzz are yours for the catching. Separate out the harsh top hairs and enjoy the soft yarn that will be in muted, elegant shades of gray and cream. Yum.

Kerry Blue Terrier (a.k.a. Irish Blue Terrier)
Named for its characteristic dark to gray-blue coat, the KBT hails from Ireland, where it was used for everything from hunting and guarding to churning butter.

Florence Richards used Keeshond and German Shepherd to create the checked blanket. (Photo courtesy of Florence Richards.)

The soft, silky hair is routinely trimmed short on much of the body, but the beast has a great undercoat. Harvest before a trip to the grooming parlor or content yourself with combings from the legs and beard. This should spin a lovely yarn.

Komondor

These beasts look like giant, rolling mops, with a fat truffle nose and lolling pink tongue attached for good measure. Unless you have a dog with a seriously flawed coat (soft and silky), your Komondor's topcoat is probably bound to its soft undercoat in dredlocklike corded tassels, creating that mop effect. Although the cords cannot be separated into spinning material, Sandra Hanson, president of the Komondor Club of America, has successfully woven cut-off cords into rugs.

Kuvasz

These large Turkish herding dogs have pure white, straight hair with longer feathering on the tail and around the neck and the croup, which is where you'll want to harvest. The good undercoat is a bit short, but definitely blendable.

Labrador Retriever

Is there a more popular all-around dog than these intelligent, sweet-tempered beasts? Everyone loves Labs—except, perhaps, anxious spinners in search of some quality fuzz. If they'd known you'd wanted it, these genial dogs undoubtedly would have tried to grow it for you. Sprinkle the short undercoat with affection, and the resulting yarn is sure to warm your heart.

Lakeland Terrier

A surprisingly soft undercoat hides beneath the hard, wiry outercoat of these mighty mites of the terrier world. It is short but can be blended with longer fibers.

Leonberger

This is a big dog—some thirty-one-and-a-half inches for the males—and there's lots of thick, fawn-colored, woolly undercoat just waiting to be combed out. This breed adores and is very protective of children, so hand your kid a comb and put him or her to work.

Sandra Hanson used Komondor cords to weave this beautiful rug. (Photo courtesy of Sandra Hanson.)

Lhasa Apso (a.k.a. Tibetan Apso)

Prized and revered by the lamas of ancient Tibet, Lhasa Apsos might well enchant the spinner in search of interesting material. The dogs have an abundant coat composed of long, straight, rough-textured hair and a shorter, softer undercoat, which spins very nicely.

Maltese (a.k.a. Melita)

Although this fluffy white beastie is a scant eight to ten inches tall, it is blessed with a luxurious quantity of long, silky, eminently spinnable hair, which is pure luxury to work with. And anyone who owns a Maltese is already grooming it with utmost care to maintain the health of its spectacular coat, so bagging the harvest should be a minor inconvenience at best. Poll your friends quickly to see if there's Maltese fuzz in your future!

Manchester Terrier

Developed in the Lancashire region of England for rabbitting and ratting, this black-and-tan dog has a short, hard, shiny coat unsuited for all but the most careful sprinkling.

Maremma

Great undercoat is available from this rare, large, Italian flock guardian/herder, but you may need to blend it with longer fibers.

Mastiff (a.k.a. Old English Mastiff)

Reputed to be an excellent guard dog (who in his right mind would presume to argue with a dog that stands some thirty inches tall?), these guys don't have any fuzz. If he wants you to collect his brushings, for heaven's sake do so and sprinkle them with longer fibers. Maybe he'd like a blanket or something.

Mexican Hairless (a.k.a. Chinese Hairless, Xoloizcuintli, Xolo)

This dog's coat is perfect for spinning the Emperor's New Clothes.

Mongrels (a.k.a. Mutts, Heinz 57-Variety, Crossbreeds)

One needn't have an impeccable lineage to be wonderfully smart, funny, courageous, or lovable—or even to be a good sport. Some of the Very Best Dogs are a wonderful mixture, exhibiting what geneticists cheerfully call "hybrid vigor." Owners of these pets will undoubtedly be able to deduce whether their dog's fuzz should be sprinkled, blended, or spun as is, before it is made into something perfectly wonderful.

Neopolitan Mastiff (a.k.a. Mastino Napolitano)

Mama Mia! Weighing in at an astonishing 150 to 200 pounds, absolutely none of it fuzz, this former fighting dog has a hard, fine coat you should sprinkle with something longer. Much longer.

Newfoundland (a.k.a. Landseer)

You could probably spin enough yarn to make a blanket from the copius coat of the gentle Newf—and what a warm blanket it would be! The outer coat is shiny, slightly oily, dense, and strong; the undercoat is thick and slightly softer. In warm climes, this courageous rescue dog

Sheila Brodeur models the sweater she created of wool and Newfoundland. (Photo courtesy of Sheila Brodeur.)

This vest is made of 100-percent Old English Sheepdog. The yarn is a lovely variegated gray.

blows its coat especially hard in the spring—give him a break and harvest frequently, he'll love you for it. Sort out the guard hairs for the softest possible yarn.

Norfolk and Norwich Terriers

These guys have typical terrier personalities—they think they can take on the big guys. The Norfolk Terrier does not produce much in the way of usable fuzz, but his wiry coat can be sprinkled amid longer fibers. The Norwich provides longer stuff, especially in the neck and shoulder area, and our blendable samples were softer than those of other terrier types, though still a bit coarse.

Old English Sheepdog (a.k.a. Bobtail)

A fuzz bonanza! Lots of shaggy stuff to work with here, and an abundant, water-proof undercoat to boot. The OES makes some very pretty yarns, as it comes in gray, blue, blue merle, and grizzle. These dogs love to run, so reward their patience during grooming with an extended romp.

Otterhound

Blessed with the movie star looks and charm of a gargantuan Benji, the Otterhound also provides the spinner with superior raw material. This rough-coated beast has a long, dense, water-proof outercoat that is hard but not wiry, and a thick, softer, oily undercoat. Either could be spun, separately or together.

Papillon (a.k.a. Butterfly Dog)

Another aristocrat's lapdog, this breed spent a great deal of time being cradled in the muffs of noblewomen; we suggest cutting to the chase and simply knitting a muff from its long, silky, thick coat—it makes storing your muff up your coat sleeve ever so much easier. Since most of your harvesting will be done from the long hairs on the tail and thighs, it may take a while to gather a sufficient quantity of fuzz. Not to worry. The naturally odor-free fuzz stores beautifully.

Pekingese (a.k.a. Foo Dog)

For centuries these dogs were the exclusive playthings of the Chinese Imperial Court, where they lived lives of unparalleled luxury. They have surprisingly coarse, thick, and long outercoats, and a softer, dense, very spinnable undercoat. The pampered Peke comes in many colors.

Petit Basset Griffon Vendéen

A diminutive descendant of the Grand Griffon Vendéen, the PBGV is the new chic dog—Mary Tyler Moore, among others, has one. This cheerful guy's harsh outercoat covers a shorter, mostly white, blendable, somewhat softer undercoat.

Pharaoh Hound

Depicted on the tombs of the great pharaohs of Egypt, these elegant hunters enjoy regular grooming with a soft brush. Trouble is, the glossy, tan hair is not good for much except sprinkling. Try mixing it with something equally rarefied, like Afghan, to preserve the beast's dignity.

Pinscher (a.k.a. German Pinscher)

Looking for all the world like a miniature Doberman Pinscher, this small dog actually preceded its more famous cousin as a breed. Other versions include the more popular Miniature Pinscher, the between-sized Harlequin Pinscher and the Swiss favorite, the Glattharidge variety. They all have the same flaw: no spinnable coat. Sprinkle with something much, much longer.

Pointer (English Pointer)

Light of foot, light of fuzz, these high-strung, hard-coated trackers can only produce sprinkles.

Polish Owczarek Nizinny (a.k.a. Pons, Polish Lowland Sheepdog)

Great spinning stuff here, even better than that of their descendants, the Bearded Collies, whom they resemble. All colors are acceptable, and since the coats must be at least four inches long before the beasts can be shown, the hair is plenty long to spin solo. Breeder Betty Augustowski has seen many items knit from dog hair in Poland, not the least of which was a Pons coat!

Polish Owczarek Podhalanski (a.k.a. Tatra or Polish Highland Sheepdog)

Another Polish entry, again rare, this dog also provides great quantities of fuzz, especially when blowing his coat. The undercoat texture is soft and woolly; the color, pure white.

Pomeranian (a.k.a. Loulou)

Queen Victoria was an early fan of the clever Pomeranian, though probably not for the same reason spinners would be: those soft, thick, fluffy undercoats! Poms come in a variety of pretty colors. Spin something as fun-loving as the beast itself.

Poodle (a.k.a. Caniche)

Poodles, which have surprisingly nice thick, fine, and woolly coats before they are shorn into topiary, come in a variety of sizes: in descending order of usefulness to the spinner, we have the standard, the miniature, and the toy. Do harvest before Fifi insists on a visit to the coiffeur, or remember to ask the hairdresser for all the lovely clippings.

Portuguese Water Dog (a.k.a. Cao de Agua)

This lively Iberian beauty comes with two distinct coat styles, although neither boasts an undercoat. The first fuzz type is slightly long, tightly crimped, softer, with a nice sheen, definitely blendable. The second is short, dense, and a good deal coarser, and may be blendable but would certainly be sprinklable.

Pug

Enormously popular with the Victorians, these peculiar-looking creatures have enjoyed favor among assorted royals for centuries. The Empress Josephine kept Pugs, as did the Duke and Duchess of Windsor. They have short, shiny, silver, apricot, or black hair, which may sprinkle but surely will not spin.

Puli

This cheerful and athletic Hungarian shepherd has a great, dense, fluffy undercoat, which could be stripped out and separated from the long, coarse outercoat. (In nature, the two tangle together in long cords; if your Puli is corded, see the Komondor entry.)

Pyrenean Shepherd Dog (a.k.a. Berger des Pyrenees)

Nearly wiped out during World War I, this small French herding dog is quick-witted and nimble, with a thick, fairly long coat. Experienced spinners will want to try to spin it solo, others may wish to blend it with a more elastic fiber.

Rhodesian Ridgeback

Named after the distinctive ridge of fur that grows along its back, this magnificent beast tackles lions and other big game in its native Africa. Its short, glossy coat is not suitable for spinning, but it would add a sprinkle of distinction to less courageous fibers.

Rottweiler

There is a very short, fine undercoat under this powerful, deep-chested dog's flat, glossy outercoat. It can be spun when mixed with longer fibers, or you could simply sprinkle it in. Much maligned in films as the quintessential "attack dog," the Rottweiler is calm and intelligent by nature—but do make sure you have his full cooperation before you pick up your brush!

Saint Bernard (a.k.a. Alpine Mastiff)

These enormously courageous mountain rescue dogs, immortalized in the film version of *Peter Pan*, have spinnable coats as well. The long-haired variety has a thick, medium-length, straight or slightly wavy coat that can be spun solo; the short-haired variety is blendable.

Saluki (a.k.a. Gazelle Hound, Persian Greyhound, Arabian Hound)

Not much to spin from this former desert hunter. It has a smooth, short, silky coat, with some feathering on the legs, ears, and thighs. The latter could be harvested slowly, and would spin a lovely, soft yarn. There's just not much of it.

This Samoyed and wool afghan was spun and knit by Colleen Milliren for Steve Gordon. (Photo courtesy of Detta Juusola; photographer, Lance Juusola.)

Samoyed

The Queen of Canine Spinnables! Siberian tribes have been spinning Samoyed hair into outerwear for centuries; it's thick, soft, and about as warm as yarn can get. It also dyes well, though we prefer its pure white, white-and-biscuit, biscuit, or cream fuzz left as pure as the heart of this hardworking beast.

Sarplaninac (a.k.a. Illyrian Sheepdog, Sar Planina)

These tall (thirty inches) Balkan flock guardians have been rendered almost extinct by the recent wars in their homeland. There are some survivors in the United States, which is good news for spinners—the mostly fawn-colored, black-masked beauties bear lots of spinnable fur.

Schipperke (a.k.a. Belgian Barge Dog)

An excellent watchdog, the lively little Schipperke has an abundant, slightly harsh outercoat. Its short, black undercoat is especially thick around the ruff of the neck and down the back of the legs and should blend nicely.

Schnauzers (Giant, Standard, and Miniature)

A lovely dense undercoat supplements the bushy outercoat, but properly groomed Schnauzers are hand-stripped to fuzz extinction! Let yours go shaggy, then strip out any spinnable fuzz. Or at least give Fido a big break between parlor visits, so you have nice, long clippings.

Scottish Terrier (a.k.a. Scottie)
The independent Scottie offers its owners a slightly coarse but spinnable undercoat, which is especially dense on the chest, belly, and legs. Although we usually think of Scotties as black, they come in a variety of colors, including sand, wheaten, gray, grizzle, and brindle.

Sealyham Terrier
Although still used for hunting in its native Wales, the Sealyham has become used to a more luxurious existence. Spinners should forego the strong, wiry outercoat for the softer undercoat, though sorting can be a chore.

Shar-Pei
With a lot more wrinkles than fuzz, this fellow was recently saved from extinction by the heroic efforts of its fanciers. However, since the Shar-Pei is prey to a host of skin problems, some of them pretty disgusting, its owners should probably not even sprinkle their mini-hairs, but content themselves with lots of photos.

Shetland Sheepdog (a.k.a. Sheltie)
Superb harvesting potential from the bright and beautiful Sheltie. Not only are these herding dogs sensitive and smart, they shed soft undercoat by the fistful! Spin something fabulous from the black, blue, merle, sable, or combination coats.

Shiba Inu
This Japanese beast, a relative of the Chow Chow, has hard, thick hair with a fine, blendable undercoat.

Shih Tzu
The Chinese so treasured this dog that they refused to sell, export, or give them to Westerners until early in this century. Spinners will treasure the lush, cottony-silky undercoat. All colors are available, and this stuff makes great yarn.

Siberian Husky
Siberians have a dense, downy undercoat that blows like a dandelion—everywhere. While you should be able to gather an impressive harvest during shedding season in the spring, the fiber is a bit short and would certainly be easier to spin combined with something a bit longer.

Silky Toy Terrier (a.k.a. Australian Silky Terrier, Silky Terrier)
Well, the name pretty much says it all. A daily brushing and combing of these blue-and-tan or gray-and-tan critters will yield long, fine straight hair, which can be harvested from all over the body. It spins a nice yarn.

Skye Terrier
Ignore the long, wiry outercoat and head straight for the soft, woolly undercoat on this appealing pet. The undercoat fibers are short, however, and you may need to combine them with something longer to make your life easier.

Sloughi (a.k.a. Arabian Greyhound, Slughi)
This aristocratic descendant of the Egyptian Greyhound has a short, fine-haired coat perfectly suited to its desert environment but a bust as fodder for a spinning wheel. With much effort, one could sprinkle the hairs amid longer fibers, although they may prove as touchy and cranky as the beast itself.

Staffordshire Bull Terrier
No way. This cross between a Bulldog and the extinct Old English Terrier has a short, smooth coat. Sprinkle carefully amid longer fibers and knit something

wonderful for your child, whom your courageous pet undoubtedly adores.

Sussex Spaniel

This is a big spaniel—some fifteen to sixteen inches tall—and he has a lovely gold-liver coat with a decent, if short, undercoat for eager harvesters. Blending works best.

Swiss Laufhund

There are four types of this Swiss hunting dog (Jura, Berner, Schweizer, and Lucerne), none of them worth a rabbit's foot as fuzz providers. Sprinkle amid longer fibers and console yourself with some truly superior Swiss chocolate.

Tibetan Spaniel

No goofier-looking than any of the other Eastern lapdogs, this little guy has a thick double coat of spinnable stuff that comes in just about every color. Do not panic if you obtain your TS as a puppy; the long coats don't show up until the third or fourth month.

Tibetan Terrier (a.k.a. Lhasa Terrier)

First of all, these guys aren't terriers—you can tell by their soft coat—but yet another breed created by those canine-loving monks in Tibet. The TT boasts a lovely, soft undercoat, which sheds yearly, and an interesting, fine, long-haired outercoat that only sheds every three years. Great stuff.

Vizsla (a.k.a. Hungarian Vizsla, Hungarian Pointer)

The wirehaired version of this smooth-coated dog offers more for the spinner to play with, but neither type will really whet your wheel, so to speak. The straight, glossy hairs are naturally oily—too bad they're so short! Sprinkle carefully.

Weimaraner

This guy comes in so many interesting shades of gray, it's a real pity the short, dense hair can only be sprinkled. Do your best, as this sensitive creature always does, and treasure the results.

Welsh Corgi

Pembroke Corgis probably entered England with Flemish weavers early in the twelfth century, though they were probably valued more as working dogs than for their thick, soft hair. The medium-length fuzz can be blended with longer fibers, which makes this dog's coat more useful for spinning than that of the Cardigan Welsh Corgi. The latter's short, wiry hair is best sprinkled and turned into something that, like these affectionate pets, travels well.

Welsh Springer Spaniel

Blessed with a short, downy innercoat and a naturally oily, silky, red-and-white outercoat of medium length, this dog provides fine blending material; a gifted spinner might be able to spin this stuff solo.

Welsh Terrier

The thick, harsh, wiry coat of this aggressive and energetic dog could be blended, but there's not much undercoat, so patience is in order.

West Highland White Terrier (a.k.a. Westies)

Since these dogs need daily grooming anyway, it isn't too much extra trouble to bag the pure-white, short undercoat to blend. Picking out the beastie's wiry topcoat can be a bit of a bore, but its devoted masters undoubtedly feel these dogs are worth it, and the outercoat is suitable only for rugs!

Wheaten Terrier (Soft-Coated)

A really pretty wheaten-colored yarn is possible from this spirited but sweet-tempered pup. The coat is properly left *au naturel,* rather than plucked, and is abundant, soft, and wavy.

Whippet
Elegant, fine-boned, faster than the town tart, but, alas, no coat. Sprinkle the fine, short hair, harvested by careful brushing, onto longer fibers and make something that, like the dog, needn't stand up to harsh weather.

Wirehaired Pointing Griffon (a.k.a. Korthals Griffon)
During shedding season, one can brush a fair amount of short, dense undercoat from these noisy, fast-paced hunting dogs. Pick out the stray harsher topcoat hairs and blend with longer fibers for the best results.

Yorkshire Terrier (a.k.a. Yorkie)
The most popular toy breed in England, the Yorkie owes its existence to a number of canine contributors—all of whom would undoubtedly be proud to claim this charming little dog as their descendant. The Yorkie boasts a long, fairly soft, spinnable coat of a particularly pretty steel blue with tan that pales to champagne toward the ends. Separate the two, or mix together for a stunning yarn.

Appendix A
Spinners for Hire

The following spinners have offered to spin pet hair for those of you who don't spin. Obviously, some of those listed are more experienced than others; we recommend asking for a small sample of yarn before you choose. Prices will vary radically as well, and do not always reflect the skill and experience of the spinner.

Many spinners will request a small sample of the animal's fur for evaluation. Your chances of having it accepted are increased a hundredfold if you have taken the time to clean it a bit—mat-free pet brushings, free of debris and foreign matter, are welcome. We received one offering containing hideous lumps of matted fur, toenails, dead bugs, and other revolting items, which had clearly been swept off a groomer's floor. Such a sample is quite likely to be rejected. The best rule of thumb is: If you don't want to touch it, they probably won't either.

One "Pet Hair from Hell" story shared by an exhausted spinner gave us pause. After agreeing to spin "some fur" for a bereft Bouvier owner, the craftsperson was the stunned recipient of three 50-pound feed sacks of fuzz, which the beast's doting owner had carefully saved over her pet's lifetime. Just when she thinks she has finally spun enough yarn, the woman woefully begs for more. The moral of the story is: Make sure both spinner and client clearly understand the precise parameters of the contract. If you don't want to spin enough yarn to blanket Dodger Stadium, for heaven's sake, say so!

ARIZONA

Helga Tirrell
2501 W. Rapallo Way
Tucson, AZ 85741
(602) 544-2205
Experienced spinner of dog hair.

CALIFORNIA

Hope F. Parshall
21500 Lassen Street
No. 145
Chatsworth, CA 91311-7208
Experienced spinning teacher and spinner of dog and cat hair, as well as other exotic fibers.

Sue Wessel
452 W. Front Street
Covina, CA 91723
Experienced pet hair spinner will spin yours.

Beatrice A. Jones
Quail Acres
Route 1, Box 434
Manton, CA 96059
Experienced spinner of pet fiber. Dog yarns tend to be firm and of fingering-weight. They are usually 3-ply and incorporate wool if they are to be used for knitting or crochet.

Janelle Embree
815 Trixis Avenue
Lancaster, CA 93534
Experienced with Samoyed dog and Angora cat hair, as well as angora rabbits. Will try other breeds.

Sandra Martin
43 Bluefield Avenue
Newbury Park, CA 91320
(805) 498-7547
Experienced dog-hair spinner; has spun Samoyed and Afghan dog hair, as well as Angora Rabbit and Buffalo but would love to try any breed.

Cindy Cates
5241 Verner Avenue
Sacramento, CA 95841
Experienced spinner welcomes opportunity to spin pet hair.

Louise O'Donnell
1358 Oakland Road
No. 17
San Jose, CA 95112
Probably the premier cat hair spinner in the U.S., Ms. O'Donnell is the only master spinner we know of to have achieved her Certificate of Excellence in feline fibers. When only the best will do. . .

COLORADO

Beverly K. Brown
65300 East 26th
Byers, CO 80103
(303) 822-5844
Experienced dog hair spinner, who does demonstrations and lessons, would be pleased to spin for you.

Mary Fitzpatrick
4900 Knox Ct.
Denver, CO 80221
(303) 480-9950
Will spin pet hair to your specifications, and will also knit items (hat, scarf, mittens, teddy bears, etc.). Flexible prices.

Pam Ramsey
La Plata Farms
1281 Country Road 123
Hesperus, CO 81326
(303) 385-4375
Experienced pet hair spinner who, we happen to know, spins gorgeous yarn, prefers to work with Collie down or Samoyed; send sample for approval. No large lots!

Marji Sinclair
201 Hankins Lane
Loveland, CO 80537
Experienced pet hair spinner will do custom work.

Connie Rudd
13456 S. Otoe Street
Pine, CO 80470
(303) 838-5961
Experienced pet hair spinner (mostly Samoyed) willing to try other breeds.

GEORGIA
Linda Jarrett
2617 Fireside Trail SW
Conyers, GA 30207
(404) 483-0671
Experienced pet hair spinner will tackle "anything!"

Paula Vester
4036 Indian Manor Drive
Stone Mountain, GA 30083
Experienced spinner is willing to spin pet fibers.

IDAHO
Elizabeth Ellis
Good Shepherd Woolworks
P.O. Box 21
Highway 93 North
Carmen, ID 83462
Will spin your dog hair for you.

IOWA
Karen S. Agee
8342 Northview Drive
Cedar Falls, IA 50613
(319) 277-1087
Experienced with Golden Retriever, various terrier and shepherd dog hair, as well as with common short-haired cat hair (which she mixes with kid mohair or wool).

ILLINOIS
Robin Hadle
5029 N. Monticello
Chicago, IL 60625
Experienced dog hair spinner will spin your fibers.

Annette Stock
1005 W. Golf Road
Mt. Prospect, IL 60056
(708) 437-9350
Spins all sorts of animal hair, from Buffalo and oxen to wolf, but has a particular preference for dog hair, particularly "Northern" breeds.

Catherine J. Brunnick
15350 E. Route 114
Momence, IL 60954
(815) 472-6911
Has spun Samoyed, Poodle, and Old English Sheepdog hair and would be pleased to spin various forms of fibers either as a sampler or as a finished product.

INDIANA
Peg Fyffe
RR 4 Box 273
Crawfordsville, IN 47933
(317) 339-4500
Award-winning spinner and knitter, experienced with both dog and cat hair, has made sweaters from both.

MASSACHUSETTS
Anita Kelman
19 Short Street
Brookline, MA 02146
Experienced spinner willing to try pet hair of your choice.

MAINE

Tracy Walk
RR 2 Box 780
Thorndike, ME 04986
Experienced spinner would love the opportunity to spin pet hair.

Sheila Brodeur
P.O. Box 184
Woolwich, ME 04579
Her specialty pet fiber is Newfoundland; contact her with other breed queries.

MARYLAND

Linda Borch
The Outback Studio
814 Annapolis Road
Gambrills, MD 21054
(410) 923-2147
Custom designer, fiber artist will spin pet hair. Has done Samoyed dog and Persian cat but will tackle anything as long as it's clean!

MICHIGAN

Sally Bartoo
943 Kensington SW
Grand Rapids, MI 49503-4827
Experienced with dog hair, this lady is willing to give any fiber a try!

Kelly M. Shively
Rocky Meadow Handspun
9003 Miller Road
Alanson, MI 49706
Experienced spinner will evaluate your fuzz for suitability and will spin that which she feels can be spun.

Carol Whitfield
1509 Glenwood Avenue
Flint, MI 48503-5517
Willing to spin pet hair, but with a real preference for dog hair!

MINNESOTA

Detta Juusola
"Detta's Spindle"
2592 Geggen-Tina Road
Maple Plain, MN 55359
(612) 479-2886
This professional spinner has made gorgeous items from pure dog hair as well as dog hair blended with other fibers. For a real treat, ask for her brochure, "Woofspuns," and see how creative you can get. She can provide a prespun, dog-wool blended yarn for the curious, and she will also custom spin your pet fiber, and/or knit or crochet it for you.

Pauline Bold
10552 Thomas Avenue S.
Bloomington, MN 55431
This experienced dog hair spinner will spin yours, too.

MONTANA

JoHanna Moebus
Box 129
Bridger, MT 59014
(406) 662-3968
This experienced pet hair spinner (dog, cat, and llama) would be delighted to "help people preserve their wonderful memories of their beloved pets."

NEW HAMPSHIRE

Mary Iselin
151 Laurel Road
Marlborough, NH 03455
(603) 876-4036
Experienced pet hair spinner will custom spin your pet hair and turn it into finished hats and/or mittens.

NEW JERSEY

Linda Mattaliano
59 First Avenue
Lindenwold, NJ 08021
(609) 627-5887

Novice spinner has already successfully spun pretty, fine yarn from her Keeshond, and will spin for you, too.

Stacy Sundance Martin
c/o Studio 14
14 Hawley Place
Willingboro, NJ 08046
This award-winning spinner and pet groomer will not only spin, weave, or knot your fiber, she can supply undercoat dog fiber as well!

NEW MEXICO
Sharon White
P.O. Box 492
Mora, NM 87732
(505) 387-5988
Experienced pet hair spinner will spin, card, knit, or weave your pet fibers, and will happily do custom orders.

NEW YORK
Cindy L. Fitzgerald
141 Munson Road
Groton, NY 13073
(607) 533-4767
Experienced dog and cat hair spinner (Samoyed, Keeshond, Pekingese, Chow, Terrier, and Himalayan and other assorted long-haired felines) willing to give yours a try. Can also blend your fibers with angora rabbit, which she raises.

Linda S. Kolassa
River Road Box 5
Westernville, NY 13486
(315) 827-4333
Experienced spinner, willing to try both dog and cat hair, any breed.

Cathy Honauer
RD 1 Box 263 Mace Hill
Middleburgh, NY 12122
(518) 827-6053
Experienced handspinner willing to spin your pet hair.

Connie Hess
P.O. Box 545
Siam Road
Windham, NY 12496
Handspinner thoroughly experienced with dog hair and some cat hair will spin your fibers, too.

NORTH CAROLINA
Bluebird Meadow Fibers
Marie Crock
623 Infinity Road
Durham, NC 27712
(919) 479-5069
This professional spinner and teacher of the craft will spin any fiber and create yarns for any project.

Merike Saarniit
Carolina Homespun
P.O. Box 687
Pleasant Garden, NC 27313
(919) 674-1190
This thoroughly experienced professional spinning teacher and weaver will spin for you, but is, in her own words, "expensive."

NORTH DAKOTA
Shannon Klein
3201 Bohnet Boulevard NE
Fargo, ND 58102
(701) 235-4543
Spinner experienced with pet hair, notably Samoyed and Old English Sheepdog, willing to spin for you.

OHIO
Diana Swords
315 Bowman Lane
Chillicothe, OH 45601
(614) 884-4237
Spinner experienced with dog, cat, angora rabbit and goat, horse and Belted Galloway cow hair seems willing to try anything!

Doris O'Donnell
Beaufait
220 W. Hines Hill Road
Boston Heights, OH 44236
(216) 463-5622
Experienced spinner has spun New-
foundland hair, as well as Buffalo and
angora rabbit.

Kelley Brandt
975 Brock-Cosmos Road
Union City, OH 45390
(513) 968-4432
Ms. Brandt spun some Newfoundland
hair for one of our promotions for this
book; she's willing to spin for you, too!

OKLAHOMA

Yvonne Collins
3121 NW73
Oklahoma City, OK 73116
Spinner interested in spinning pet hair.

Nina M. Koelsch
Fiberrifics . . . fiber to finish
6154 S. 80th West Avenue
Tulsa, OK 74131
(918) 445-5220/445-1630
Enthusiastic handspinner who "enjoys
spinning unusual things" has tackled
qiviut, camel down, yak, and horse as
well as more conventional fibers, and
recently completed a scarf made from
chow "down," for a client.

OREGON

Victoria Downing
60656 Gosney Road
Bend, OR 97702
(503) 382-6593
Experienced dog hair spinner (Golden
Retriever, Shetland Sheepdog, Wolf, etc.)
will happily do yours as well.

Sandra McDonald
RAINCROFT
47993 Floras Lk. Lp.
Langlois, OR 97450
(503) 348-2550
Another exotic fiber specialist with qiviut,
yak down, and camel down to her credit,
not to mention rabbit, cat, and dog, she is
"willing to tackle anything," and even
offers a money-back guarantee. Custom
knitting also available, and she can
arrange to have your fibers woven as well.

PENNSYLVANIA

Pat Campbell
Angora Hollow Farm
RD 2, Box 317B
Oley, PA 19547
(215) 987-6599
Experienced pet hair spinner will spin
yours.

Lynn Holdsworth
Stonyfield Farm
310 Legion Heights
Elkland, PA 16920
(814) 258-5369
Experienced spinner with scouring and
carding service "have wheel—will spin—
just about anything!" Will also knit items.

Karen Klaiber
RD 2, Box 88A
Kane, PA 16735
(814) 837-6076
Experienced pet hair spinner (Samoyed,
Sheltie, Golden Retriever, and Collie) will-
ing to try anything.

Doreen Malone
RD 2, Box 88
Kane, PA 16735
(814) 837-8514
Another Samoyed spinner willing to try
other breeds for you.

SOUTH DAKOTA

Marjorie Hayes
1423 N. 3rd
Aberdeen, SD 57401
(605) 225-1352
Pet hair spinner willing to do yours, too!

TENNESSEE

Anne Foley
2061 King College Road
Bristol, TN 37620
Experienced dog and cat hair spinner (Black Chow Chow, Norwegian Elkhound and long-haired Siamese cat, among others) willing to spin for you.

TEXAS

Carolyn Bush
9535 Riverton Avenue
Dallas, TX 75218-2755
This expert dog and cat hair spinner will not only spin your pet's fur, but will needlepoint his or her likeness and fashion it into a framed picture or a pillow. Her work is truly extraordinary.

VIRGINIA

Barbara Tinder
Carolton Farm and Fiber
5401 Carolton Lane
Barboursville, VA 22923
(703) 672-2935
This experienced spinner will spin, dye, weave, and knit for you.

Barbara S. Gentry
Stony Mountain Fibers
West End—Downtown Mall
104 Old Preston Avenue
Charlottesville, VA 22901
(804) 295-2008
This professional spinning teacher would like to see your pet fiber, but can be persuaded to spin it if it has been washed, picked, and carded.

Brenda D. Collins
Fiber Artist
P.O. Box 184
Fincastle, VA 24090
(703) 473-1201
Will spin, knit, and weave any and all pet fibers. Can sprinkle, blend, and spin, as your pet's coat requires and you request.

N. Margand
508 Jackson Avenue
Lexington, VA 24450
Although this spinner is experienced with dog fiber, notably Border Collie and Samoyed, allergies prevent her from working with cats! She will spin any dog hair.

Bobbie Geyer
7417 Colton Lane
Manassas, VA 22110
(703) 257-7653
This Samoyed specialist has also spun (and will spin) other pet fibers, and also does custom knitting and weaving.

Sherry Blanchette
P.O. Box 251
Lovingston, VA 22949
Will spin pet hair—all work done on a drop spindle, which she feels is "more authentic, old-fashioned, it delivers a heavier yarn than spinning wheels do."

Susan B. Alkhadra
6621 Hidden Woods Court
Roanoke, VA 24018
(703) 389-0336
This willing canine fiber spinner will spin your pooch, too.

WASHINGTON

Pat Galloway
P.O. Box 3244
Arlington, WA 98223
Experienced dog hair spinner, who recently spun yarn for a bereaved Samoyed owner, finds pet hair spinning

"very satisfying, knowing how much this means (to the owner) from an emotional point of view."

Laurie Nix-Mayer
Pet Fuzzies
25325 SE 133 Rd.
Issaquah, WA 29027
(206) 392-6284
Experienced pet hair spinner will spin, knit, and crochet for you.

Kim Zydek
840 Cinebar Road
Cinebar, WA 98533
This skilled spinner has experience with all manner of animal fibers, and is especially interested in fine spinning.

Carolyn Smith
Creative Comforts Handspinning & Garment Design
P.O. Box 606
Vashon Island, WA 98070
(206) 463-2004
This handspinning professional has knitting patterns for dog hair, in addition to her carding service. She will spin your fiber and help you design something wonderful from it.

Denise M. Bresee
122 Hemlock Drive
Chehalis, WA 98532
(206) 748-1797
Spinner experienced with conventional fibers and short-haired tabby cat, is eager to try dog hair as well.

WEST VIRGINIA
Elizabeth Davis
Route 1, Box 180-C
Bridgeport, WV 26330-9374
(304) 842-5080
Spinner willing to spin your pet hair.

The Barefoot Spinner
Maureen Pritchard
HC 79 Box 31-A
Romney, WV 26757
(304) 822-5767
Professional spinner will spin and knit all pet fibers.

WISCONSIN
Kathy Foster
Fiberbits Farm
S104 W38751 Highway NN
Eagle, WI 53119
In addition to raising sheep, llamas, and angora rabbits, this spinning teacher sells animal fiber and is experienced with dog fiber, especially Great Pyrenees. She will also weave.

Joslyn Seefeldt
5738 Klug Road
Milton, WI 53563
(608) 868-4070
Experienced pet hair spinner (especially Samoyed, from which she has knit sweaters) can do straight or blended fibers for you, too.

Appendix B
Sources of Supplies

We have included the following list of suppliers to help you get started, but it is by no means complete—check your yellow pages under "crafts," "yarns," or even "spinning," and consult periodicals such as *Shuttle, Spindle and Dyepot,* published by The Handweavers Guild of America (2402 University Avenue, Suite 702, Minneapolis, MN 55114 [612] 646-0802) or *Spin-Off,* published by Interweave Press, Inc. (201 East Fourth Street, Loveland, Colorado 80537 [303] 669-7672) or *Heddle* (Box 1906, Bracebridge, Ontario, P0B 1 C0 Canada).

SPINNING WHEELS AND EQUIPMENT

Ashford produces a comprehensive line of spinning products, including wheels.

For the dealer nearest you, write:

Crystal Palace Yarns
3006 San Pablo Avenue
Dept 6, Berkeley, CA 94702

Forestville Wheels
P.O. Box 1296
Forestville, CA 95436

Clemes & Clemes
650 San Pablo Ave.
Pinole, CA 94564
(510) 724-2036

SPINNING WHEELS, DRUM CARDERS, DROP SPINDLES, ETC.

Schacht Spindle Co. produces a variety of spinning equipment. To contact the dealer nearest you, write:

Schacht Spindle Co.
6101 Ben Place
Boulder, CO 80301

Norsk Fjord Fiber
P.O. Box 271-so
Lexington, GA 30648
Nordic tools, nostepinners, waisthooks, viking wool combs.

Yarn Barn
918 Massachusetts
Lawrence, KS 66044
Spinning supplies, comprehensive.

The Country Craftsman Spinning Wheel
Dept. S, P.O. Box 412
Littleton, MA 01460
(508) 486-4053
Write for the dealer nearest you.

Evergreen Enterprises Inc.
267 Burt Street
Taunton, MA 02780
(508) 823-2377
*Fiber art equipment
Ashford, Louet and Country Craftsman, spinning wheels.*

The Sheep Shed
Bellairs Hillside Farm
8351 Big Lake Rd.
Clarkston, MI 48346
(313) 625-2665
Spinning supplies, wheels.

Detta's Spindle
2592 Geggan-Tina Rd.
Maple Plain, MN 55359
(612) 479-2886
Schact, Reeves, Majacraft, Country Craftsman, Jensen, Ashford, and Louet wheels, as well as one of the most knowledgeable women in the business to advise you.

Rio Grande Weaver's Supply
216-B Pueblo Norte
Taos, NM 87571
(505) 758-0433
Carries the Rio Grande Wheel.

Carolina Homespun
P.O. Box 687
Pleasant Garden, NC 27313
(919) 674-1190
Ashford, Louet, Reeves, Schacht, and Timbertops wheels, comprehensive catalog of combs, looms, etc.

Earth Guild
33 Haywood Street
Dept. SSD
Asheville, NC 28801
1 (800) 327-8448
Weaving, spinning, and dyeing tools, materials, and books.

The Woolroom
Laurelton Rd. S
Mt. Kisko, NY 10549
Curry wheels, Schacht, Lendrum, Reeves, Louet, Ashford. Catalog.

Creek Water Wool Works
P.O. Box 716
Salem, OR 97308
(503) 585-3302
Ashford, Country Craftsman, Haldane, Lendrum, Louet, Reeves, and Schacht Wheels, handcrafted by Van Eaton, and other supplies.

Wooly & Wilds
Dept. S4 HC 71
125 Radar Hill Rd.
Burns, OR 97720
(503) 573-4203
Lots of fiber equipment, Ashford, Schacht, Louet, Lendrum, etc., wheels.

Bauernhof Fiber
P.O. Box 1286
Cave Junction, OR 97523
Handcrafted Saxony wheels.

Woodland Woolworks
17340 NE Woodland Loop
Yamhill, OR 97148-8420
1 (800) 547-3725

Ashford, Country Craftsman, Elec spinner (sic) Lendrum, Louet, Majacraft, and Schacht wheels, full line of fiber equipment.

J. A. Meck
P.O. Box 756
Cornelius, OR 97113
English paddle combs.

The Mannings
1132 Green Ridge Rd.
P.O. Box 687
East Berlin, PA 17316
Spinning wheels and hard-to-find equipment; catalog available.

Suzanne Roddy, Handweaver
1519 Memorial Drive
Conroe, TX 77304
(409) 756-1719
Catalog. Special orders, many wheels available.

Stony Mountain Fibers
West End—Downtown Mall
104 Old Preston Ave.
Charlottesville, VA 22901
Comprehensive spinning equipment.

Misty Mountain Farm
Rte. 1 Box 341
Delaplane, VA 22025
(703) 364-1947
Spinning and weaving equipment, Louet, Reeves, and Ashford wheels, catalog.

Mountain Loom Co.
Box 1107, Castle Rock, WA 98611
1 (800) 238-0296
Carries the Roberta electronic spinner by Ertoel Wheels.

Susan's Fiber Shop
N. 250 HWY A
Columbus, WI 53925
(414) 623-4237
Viking combs, board carders, English 5

pitch combs, minicombs, wheels, looms, lots of stuff.

The Spinning Wheel Shop
1135 Highway K
Wisconsin Dells, WI 53965
(608) 254-2605
Single and double treadle wheels crafted from northern hardwoods.

CANADA AND FOREIGN
Louet
RR 4 Dept. 112
Prescott, Ontario
Canada K0E 1T0
(613) 925-4502
Louet spinning equipment is sold throughout the U.S. and Canada. Contact the home office for the dealer nearest you.

Lendrum Folding Spinning Wheels
RR 4 Odessa
Ontario, Canada K0H 2H0
(613) 386-7151
Majacraft spinning wheels are sold by dealers throughout the U.S. To contact the dealer nearest you, write:
Majacraft
Munro Rd.
RD 6 Tauranga New Zealand
0064-7-5524672

Timbertops
Wheel Lodge
159 Main Street
Asfordby, Melton Mowbray, Leics.
LE14 3TS, U.K.
0664-812320

CARDERS
Patrick Green Carders
48793 Chilliwack Lake Road
Sardis, B.C. V2R 2P1 Canada
(604) 858-6020

CUSTOM CARDING

Good Shepherd Woolworks
P.O. Box 21
Highway 93 N
Carmen, ID 83462
Will process your dog hair for you!

Sullivan's Springwater Spinoffs
26045 S. Warnock
Estacada, OR 97023
(503) 630-4520

Ohio Valley Natural Fibers
8541 Louderback Rd.
Sardinia, OH 45171-9603
*Nothing is too strange for these folks to
tackle: they regularly do "rover rovings"
and would be delighted to card your dog
fiber, too! Will also spin it for you.*

Frankenmuth Woolen Mill & Sweater
Store
570 S. Main Street
Frankenmuth, MI 48734
(517) 652-8121
*Will wash, pick, and card your dog hair
into rovings for you to spin, or for you to
send to a spinner who would rather not
do all the prep work!*

DYES

Country Classics Dyes
G & K Craft Ind. Ltd.
P.O. Box 38
Somerset, MA
(508) 676-3980

Pro Chemical and Dye Co.
P.O. Box 14
Somerset, MA 02726-0014
1 (800) 2 BUY DYE

Aljo Dyes
81 Franklin Street
New York, NY 10013
(212) 226-2878
(212) 966-4046
Gaywool Dyes
Nooramunga Road
Devenish Vic. 3726 Australia
Phone: 011 61 57 641363
Fax: 011 61 57 641322

IN THE UNITED STATES:

Warehouse Gaywool Dyes
26434 189th Ave., SE
Kent, WA 98042
Ph/fax (206) 631-7364

Glossary of Terms

Blending: The process of combining fibers before spinning. Dog fibers between one and two inches long should be blended with longer fibers to facilitate spinning. (For even shorter fibers, see *Sprinkling.*) Dog fibers can also be blended with wool to provide greater elasticity in the finished yarn.

Blowing Coat: The precipitous shedding of vast quantities of pet fibers, not to be confused with ongoing shedding. Dogs usually "blow their coats" in the spring, and to a lesser extent in the fall. This is the perfect time to collect your pet's fuzz, as you could do irreparable damage to the average vacuum cleaner if you attempted to rid your home of this prodigious output in the traditional manner.

Bobbin: The cylindrical piece of the spinning wheel on which spun yarn is wound.

Brushings: Fibers collected by grooming your pet. This is the preferred method of harvesting fibers for spinning.

Carding: The process of untangling and aligning fibers prior to spinning, carding works on the same principle as brushing one's hair. While carding is required if the fibers have been washed, and is recommended for clippings, one can spin brushings "straight from the dog" without carding. The tools for carding are carders or carding combs.

Clippings: Fibers that have been separated from the dog with the aid of scissors. Many clippings yield a prickly yarn because the cut end of the fiber tends to stick out from the finished yarn. Many Poodle clippings, however, produce quite a soft yarn, which is pretty convenient since so many Poodles are clipped.

Double Coat: Describes coats that have fibers of two distinct textures, with the length of the fibers and often the color being quite different. Dogs such as Golden Retrievers and Collies are said to be double-coated. (See also *Single Coat* and *Undercoat*.)

Drafting: The action of pulling fibers out from the mass of fibers to be spun in preparation for twisting them into yarn.

Exotic Fibers: Generally used to refer to nonsheep spinnables such as cashmere, alpaca, vicuña, and so forth. Pet fibers are more similar to these fibers than they are to wool in their spinning characteristics and in the soft, fuzzy yarn they produce.

Felting: The process of creating felt fabric from wool or other fibers, this is achieved by heating and cooling fibers in sequential baths. It is desirable when one *wants* felt as an end product, but a major disaster when one is attempting to wash fibers in order to spin them—hence the caution to wash and rinse fibers in lukewarm water and avoid sudden changes in water temperature.

Fiber: The material that formerly resided on the dog, the sheep, the cotton plant, etc. that one might like to spin. We find the term a little cold, and often use the more user-friendly and descriptive "fuzz."

Fun Fur: A politically correct garment somewhat resembling a fur coat but created without harm to the donor critter. The ultimate product of knitting with dog hair.

Fuzz Balls (also Fuzz Bunnies, Fur Balls, Fur Puffs, etc.): You'll know 'em if you've got 'em, and if you have a shedder and don't have a maid, undoubtedly you've got 'em. These are the tumbleweedlike collections of fuzz from which your dog has parted and which currently reside under all the furniture in your house. Under certain circumstances (for instance, when you are very busy writing a book), these can grow to gargantuan proportions.

Fuzz: Our affectionate catch-all term for dog fibers, it most accurately refers to

the soft undercoat, rather than to the coarser, more hairlike fibers that comprise many dog coats.

Gauge: The calculation of how many stitches per inch a particular yarn yields on a particular size needle. No knitting directions would be complete without a stern admonishment to "check your gauge," but it is even more important with hand-spun yarn than it is with store-bought yarn. Please do check your gauge—it's the right thing to do.

Guard Hairs: The coarser hairs that comprise the outercoat of some double-coated dogs. These are not ideal for spinning and should be separated from the softer fibers before spinning.

Guide Hooks: The parts of the spinning wheel through which the yarn is threaded to help it wind on the bobbin evenly.

Halo: The characteristic "fuzziness" apparent in garments made from dog yarn, mohair, or angora.

Harvesting: Our fond term for collecting dog fibers, whether by brushing, clipping, or just looking under the furniture. "Collecting" seems to us to connote simply hoarding, while "harvesting" includes the sense of doing something really useful with the stuff in the near future.

Lazy Kate: A tool used for plying, the lazy kate simply holds two or more bobbins of yarn, allowing them to unwind without tangling. Frankly, a couple of jars on the floor do the trick just as well, but it's almost worth buying a lazy kate just because it has such a great name. (See also *Niddy-Noddy*.)

Leader Yarn: The yarn attached to the spindle or spinning wheel and onto which one begins spinning one's own yarn.

Niddy-Noddy: Another spinning tool with a truly splendid name, the niddy-noddy is used to wind skeins of yarn. While not an essential tool, it is a help in making skeins of a consistent length.

Orifice: Another part of a spinning wheel, this is the hole through which the finished yarn is drawn onto the bobbin.

Outercoat: One portion of the coat on a double-coated dog. The opposite of outercoat is undercoat, not innercoat. The outercoat is almost invariably coarser than the undercoat, and therefore less desirable for spinning. (See also *Guard Hairs*.)

Petspun: Our affectionate term for yarn made from pet fibers, it is etymologically related to "hand-spun" or "homespun."

Plying: The process of twisting two or more strands of yarn together to create a heavier, stronger yarn. Plying can be done on a spinning wheel or with a drop spindle, and is usually accomplished by twisting the fibers together in the opposite direction than they were initially spun. Strands of the same fibers can be plied or, for example, a strand of petspun can be plied with a strand of wool.

Rake: A dog-grooming tool, available in most pet stores, designed to remove the undercoat. (See *Stripping*.) Please do not use a garden rake on your dog under any circumstances.

Rolag: A sausage-shaped collection of fibers ready to be spun. Rolags are created by rolling a pad of carded fibers off the carder.

Shedder: A formerly perjorative term for a pet with a tendency to leave vast quantities of hair all over one's home. Now used to describe the supremely desirable animal companion.

Shedding: What the shedder does when he is anxious to share with you the fruits of his follicles.

Sheep: Once much sought after for their fleece, this species is soon to be obsolete to everyone except, perhaps, lamb chop connoisseurs.

Single Coat: Describes coats comprised of fibers of a uniform texture. Single-coated

dogs include Afghans and Great Danes. (See also *Double Coat*.)

Skein: A neat package of yarn created by winding yarn into a large loop and tying it in several places. Yarn can be washed or dyed in skein form, and should be stored in skein form until ready to use to avoid stretching. "Skein" is also a verb meaning to make one.

Slicker Brush: A dog-grooming tool available at pet stores, the slicker brush is a cross between a comb and a brush, with lots of tiny wire teeth.

Spindle: A tool used for spinning. A simple drop spindle can be made using scraps of wood.

Spinning: The process of transforming fibers into a continuous strand of yarn.

Sprinkling: Our term for a method of combining very short dog fibers (for example, Beagle, Boxer) with longer fibers. This method is only for the truly obsessed, those determined to have a memento of a cherished short-haired pet. We recommend sprinkling pet fibers onto fibers of a contrasting color so that you're sure to see the tiny bits that came from Bubbles. (See also *Blending*.)

Stripping: Removing much of the dog's undercoat. Groomers often use a rake or a stripping knife to strip a coat.

Treadle Wheel: A popular type of spinning wheel. The wheel is driven by the foot, leaving both hands free for the action of spinning.

Treadling: The heel-to-toe action of driving a treadle wheel with the foot. We recommend practicing treadling without spinning until it is second-nature.

Undercoat: The opposite of outercoat, this is the portion of a double coat lying closest to the dog's skin. This is generally the softest and finest fiber in the coat, with a fluffy and downy texture, and is the most desirable for spinning.

Warp: A weaving term. The warp is the lengthwise yarn that is stretched on the loom before weaving. Warp should be smooth and very strong, and we do not generally recommend using dog fibers on warp. (See also *Woof.*)

Wiry: Describes a coat comprised of fairly stiff, hairlike fibers. Most of the terriers have wiry coats. While this material is spinnable, the yarn it produces is scratchy.

Woof (also Weft): A weaving term for the yarn that is woven width-wise among the warp fibers on the loom. Dog yarn is recommended for use as woof rather than warp. "Woof" is also what one's dog is likely to say when he sees the sweater you made from his yarn.

Conversion Tables

*KNITTING NEEDLE
CONVERSION CHART*

Continental (mm.)	British	U.S.
2.25	13	0
2.75	12	1
3	11	2
3.25	10	3
3.75	9	4
4	8	5
4.5	7	6
5	6	7
5.5	5	8
6	4	9
6.5	3	10
7	2	10.5
7.5	1	11
8.5	00	13
9	000	15

METRIC/IMPERIAL
CONVERSION CHART

Please note that these conversions are *approximate*
to the nearest quarter inch.

cm.	in.	cm.	in.
1	½	19	7½
2	¾	20	7¾
3	1¼	21	8¼
4	1½	22	8¾
5	2	23	9
6	2¼	24	9½
7	2¾	25	9¾
8	3¼	26	10¼
9	3½	27	10¾
10	4	28	11
11	4¼	29	11½
12	4¾	30	11¾
13	5	31	12¼
14	5½	32	12½
15	6	33	13
16	6¼	34	13½
17	6¾	35	13¾
18	7	36	14¼

Index of Breeds